James Hillman

Insearch

PSYCHOLOGY AND RELIGION

SECOND REVISED EDITION
featuring a Preface and Postscript
by the Author

Spring Publications Woodstock, Connecticut

THE JUNGIAN CLASSICS SERIES 2

Second printing of revised edition 1995 by Spring Publications, Inc.,
299 East Quassett Rd., Woodstock, CT 06281. Typography of the 1967
original edition is reproduced by permission of Charles Scribner's Sons,
New York. Printed in the United States of America. Cover designed and
produced by Margot McLean and Slobodan Trajkovic. Text printed on
acid free paper

Distributed in the United States by the Continuum Publishing Group;
in Canada by McClelland and Stewart; in the United Kingdom, Eire, and
Europe by Airlift Book Co.; in Austrailia by Astam Books Pty Ltd; in
Europe by Daimon Verlag; and in South Africa by Feffer and Simons

Library of Congress Cataloging-in-Publication Data

Hillman, James.
    Insearch : psychology and religion / James Hillman.— 2nd rev.
    ed. / featuring a preface and postscript by the author.
        p.   cm. — (The Jungian classics series ; 2)
    Includes bibliographical references.
    ISBN 0-88214-512-6 (pbk. : alk. paper)
    I. Pastoral psychology. 2. Psychoanalysis and religion. 3. Jung,
    C.G. (Carl Gustav), 1875-1961. I Title.   II. Series.
    BV4012.H5 1994
    253.5'2—dc20   94-24835
                                                          CIP

Preface to the 1994 Edition

FOR THIS new edition of a book first written some thirty years ago I have added a Postscript in the form of a critical review. This deconstructive move, appropriate to the nineties, completes the hermeneutic circle: author as critic of his own work. The critique intends three main tasks.

I want to place the book in the context of its time, the mid-sixties; I want to expose the close relation of classical Jungian thought and Christian pastoral care. And, I want to comment on the contemporary nineties' fascination with soul in which this book partakes.

For this is primarily a book of soul—soul as conceived and expressed within the traditional language of our Western history, which is inescapably Christian. So we find the following pages speak of God, not Gods; God as a He, not a She; God as Love, and many passing references to Christ and the Bible.

Perhaps this confluence of its rhetoric with mainstream feeling and that this book does not truly conflict with half-conscious attitudes shared by the culture account for its continued success. For it goes on selling and selling, and finds ever new uses

3

as a teaching text in Jungian study groups, introductory courses, and seminaries.

Readers who know my later work wonder how this book fits in—even how it could possibly have been written at all by an author so dedicated to the polytheism of Mediterranean paganism and his "Running Engagement with Christianity," the phrase I used as a chapter title in *Inter Views* (1983) and explained with some care in a chapter of *The Dream and the Underworld* (1979). In these two places I laid out my critique, woven all through my post-*Insearch* writings, of the unconscious Christian dogmas and fantasies that severely impede deeper psychological understanding—a point made years ago by Nietzsche, Freud, and also Jung.

The Postscript attempts both a critique of the book and a justification of its Christianism. For the Christian influence leaves its mark on all that its pages say about soul, about love, evil, therapy, religion, and the nature of human personality. The style itself echoes with inspiring homiletics, practical sermonizing, and the high seriousness of redemptive purpose, all in the guise of the Jungian feeling function.

I wish for *Insearch* that the values its readers have found—readers also in Dutch, German, Italian, Japanese, and Portuguese—will go on being of service. Toilers in the common field of counseling and therapy, because of their feeling for and understanding of the soul's fantastic labyrinth, are inevitably led ever deeper in search of insights and images to enliven their work.

Thompson CT, Summer 1994   J. H.

Prefatory Note

THE ORIGINS of this small book are several. During the last few years, through analytical work and friends among clergy of different denominations, I have been engaged more and more with problems of religion and psychology. The nucleus of these chapters consists of lectures given by invitation to ministers concerned with analytical psychology and pastoral counseling. Because the new theology and new morality as developed through the *Honest to God* debate have repercussions within psychology, questions must be put. Also, the implications of a theology that has become a theo-thanatology, or a study of a "dead" God, and which demythologizes religion must be faced since analytical psychology tends to have just the reverse effect. It moves toward "re-mythologizing" experiences with religious implications, as the following pages try to show. Major emotional ideas, such as the idea and image of God, can "die" out of psychic life, but not for long. The energy bound to these complex ideas and feelings does not just vanish, much as man might like to free himself of the burdensome notion of God by writing theological obituaries.

For psychology the issue is not that "God is dead," but in what forms this indestructible energy is now reappearing in the psyche. What can the psyche tell us about the direction religion might take now? In what images will that major emotional idea of God be reborn?

My main concern, however, was to give the feel of analytical experience in its relevancy for counseling. Counseling depends as much upon the practitioner's psychology as upon his theology, and to this psychology analysis may make a contribution. My attempts to contribute may fall outside the usual lines of professional psychological advice, because I have come to believe that pastoral work, rather than attempting clinical sophistication, could go further and deeper and could reach more people were it to develop within its own vital tradition. This leads straight to the psychological problem of reconnecting with this tradition. Although a psychological problem, it is at the same time for each of us—especially for the minister—a major religious problem: the search for the soul and the belief in its reality, which means finding a living connection to one's own psychic reality. Here, analytical psychology can contribute.

Pastoral counselors have been partly led astray in the way in which they have taken to psychology. The word "clinical" has become all but numinous; a minister's visit is a "housecall"; parishioners are "patients"; psychodynamic cure tends to replace psychological care. Yet the deep need of the individual remains. Although his need is less for mental health than for guidance of soul, he still turns to his analyst for what he might be receiving from his minister, so that analyst and minister seem each to be performing the other's task. The minister has held back from fulfilling his model of shepherd of souls, because he has felt himself to be an amateur who "hadn't enough psychology." But he has his own psyche out of which comes his own calling and his insight into others. Is not the psychological amateur, truly defined as the

6

one who lovingly cultivates the soul, anyway the true psychological specialist? For him, clinical psychopathology and programs of research will yield less than his own individual insearch.

As these chapters now stand they are addressed no longer to the minister only, since the living experience of psychic reality is but a way of describing the soul, and the inner life of the psyche is not only a professional matter. The counselor, responsible for souls by his pastoral vocation, has to face its trials daily and so the discussion in these pages is primarily with him. But the book can no more be restricted to him alone than can religion and psychology be concerns only for professional theologians and psychologists.

The gradual replacement of "soul" by "psyche" in this century and the consequent professionalism in dealing with its troubles are beginning to do as much damage as did the ignorance and moralisms about the psyche in the last century. As psyche cannot replace the soul, professionalism cannot substitute for vocation. So I would be pleased if these pages helped to free us from professionalism about the soul and toward returning its care to the pastoral counselor as well as to any individual who is lay in the sense of open and who is moving along the frontiers of contemporary insearch.

September 1967   J. H.

Contents

Psychological work. Expectations, needs, and demands. Ego intentions of the counselor. Listening.
Ear as organ of consciousness. Curiosity. Confession.
Psychological testing as form of curiosity. Secrecy
and natural distance. Psychological space in the encounter. Human encounter constellates archetype of
love. Love as activity and as state of being. Human
encounter and inner connection. Inner vertical connection balances outer relationships. Intimacy and
community.

Analysis and theology meet in the soul. "Soul" as
concept. "Loss of soul." Soul is not mind; pastoral

counseling is not psychotherapy. The soul and the counselor's calling. Theology and depth psychology place soul "within" and "below." Soul and the unconscious. "Proofs" of the unconscious. Complexes. Moods. Symptoms. Dreams. Befriending the dream. Understanding the dream. Awakening of inner life. Religious concern of the soul. Reality of inner world. Rediscovery of inner myth and religion.

Splits between preaching and practice, between pulpit and analytical chair. Morality of analysis. Inner darkness as the repressed and forgotten and as the potential and germinating. Images of the shadow. Moral struggles. "Cure" of the shadow. Paradox of loving and judging. Moral code of analysis as container for personality development. Bishop Robinson and the "new morality." Naïve view of love in *Honest to God.* Analytical morality and the intensification of conflict. Internalization of eros. Spiritual idealism and psychological disciplines. Transcendent background of the moral impulse. Conscience. Self-regulation. The Devil and archetypal evil. Shadow in the counselor. Morality and feeling.

Feminine images in the masculine psyche. Anima figures and their effects. Emotions and moods: self-pity, sentimentality, sadness. The feminine side in comparative religion: the Shaman, Greek heroes, Hinduism, the Buddha, Judeo-Christian tradition. Mary and the Annunciation. Cultivation of eros within. Problems of sexual love. Marriage. Fantasy, reflection, imagination, and the sacrifice of ego-activity. Flesh and body. Psychosomatics. Union with the body and the "sister." The feminine ground of the religious moment.

"A wise man's heart inclines him toward the right,
but a fool's heart toward the left."

ECCLESIASTES 10:2

" . . . let him become a fool that he may become wise."

1 CORINTHIANS 3:18

I

HUMAN ENCOUNTERS

AND THE INNER

CONNECTION

To BE in a human world is to live in a world of humans, and in a sense what more occupies our lives than people? From the beginning we emerge into awareness within a web of human connections which unceasingly engage us until death. It is not merely that man is a social being but that his nature as human implies a life of feeling and encounters with others. Work, art, nature, and ideas may take us with them for a while, but soon we are back immersed in "real life"—and real life means simply the human being, ourselves, and other people. In these encounters with ourselves and with others, we fail and are failed. As time goes on, the mounting tragedy over what happens in life means in part what God, fate, and circumstances have brought about, but more it means what happens in the relationships with other people. Here we

15

believe ourselves responsible. Things could have been different had we but known better, been more conscious, understood more psychology.

The analyst or counselor is called upon when human encounters become destructive and insupportable. Our work seems to begin with the shadows which fall between people. We are supposed to be the specialists about human problems. However, human problems are not something people have, but something people are. The problem in psychology is the individual himself, just as I am my own problem. In our work, the patient is the disease itself, so that the cure may never be its riddance but is the care of the person whom we meet.

Psychological work begins with the human meeting. What we know and have read, our gifts of intelligence and character—all we have gained through training and experience leads to this moment. Where the encounter fails, all falls flat: two people in two chairs talking, trying. If all our work begins here, then let us begin with an attempt to put some light upon some of the dark areas between two people, especially upon those shadows which prevent counseling.

Communication, dialogue, interpersonal relations are voguish topics. There are enough theories; academic proliferation and escalation are evils of the day. Rather let us discuss the shadows of counseling in the actual encounter. These shadows are less something that happens between people than they are something that happens within each person. If therefore any improvement is to come about in our work we are obliged to look within ourselves. Psychology cannot avoid beginning within the psychologist.

Analysts, counselors, social workers are all trouble-shooters and problem-solvers. We are looking for trouble, even before a person comes in to take the waiting chair: "What's the matter?" "What's wrong?" The meeting begins not only with the projections of the person coming for help, but with the trained and organized intention of the professional helper. In analysis we would say that the countertransference is there before the transference begins. My expectations are there with me as I wait for the knock on the door.

In fact, countertransference is there from the beginning since some unconscious call in me impels me to do this work. I may bring to my work a need to redeem the wounded child, so that every person who comes to me for help is my own hurt childhood needing its wounds bound up by good parental care. Or the reverse: I may be still the wonderful son who would lead his father or mother out of the mistaken ways of their night-wood, bringing them light and renewal. This same parent-child archetype may also affect us, for instance, in the need to correct, even punish, parents, extending as far as the need to correct and punish an entire older generation, its ideals and values.

My needs are never absent. I could not do this work did I not need to do this work. But my needs are not mine alone; at a deeper level they belong to, reflect, and speak from a situation which corresponds as well with the other's needs. Just as the person who comes to me needs me for help, I need him to express my ability to give help. The helper and the needy, the social worker and the social case, the lost and the found, always go together.

However, we have been brought up to deny our needs. The ideal man of western protestantism shows his "strong ego" in independence. To need is to be dependent, weak; needing implies submission to another. Discussion of what this attitude does to the weaker and more feminine side of the person we shall have to reserve to the last chapter. But here it is necessary to note that needs and calls hardly differ. The call tends to be experienced as coming more from without the personality, whereas needs seem "mine," coming from within. To deny a call is indeed dangerous, for it is a denial of one's essence which is transpersonal. But is not the denial of a need equally dangerous? Needs are not only personal. There is a level to them which is objective, so that, for instance, the need I feel to be with you is not only my personal need but the objective requirement of the relationship we have, the voice which asks that it be kept alive. Need makes us human; if we did not need one another, if we could meet and satisfy our own needs, there would be no human society. Although I cannot meet my own needs, I may be able to meet yours. Although I cannot understand myself, I can help understand you, as you can me. This reciprocity is part of the mutual using and giving of love.

Needs in themselves are not harmful, but when they are denied they join the shadows of counseling and work from behind as demands. A counselor may need to instruct and educate, to teach what he knows, because it fulfills an essential part of himself. It evokes his specific call into action. Yet he can hardly demand that each person coming to him each visit come only for instruction. His need to teach may have to find other fulfillment, else it may become an unconscious demand on each person who comes to him. If I admit my need for analytical work, I may demand less from those who come. Because demands build up when needs are not admitted, acknowledgment of my needs subjectively, as a fact of my humanity, my dependent creatureliness, will help to prevent these same needs from degenerating into demands for actual fulfillment upon the objective world. Demands ask for fulfillment, needs require only expression.

Besides the need for trouble, another main call to this kind of work is the need for intimacy. Not everyone has a predilection for close personal revealing conversation. If I am unaware of this need for intimacy, and I am not tending to it within the other contexts of my life, it may turn into a demand upon the other person, even into a demand upon myself, so that I become over-revealing and over-personal about

18

myself, turning the therapeutic hour into a mutual confession.

The dominant figures of our culture may influence our work, so that any of us engaged in teaching and healing, whether in the church or not, Christian or not, may be identified with aspects of the archetypal image of Christ. This identification may show, for instance, with those who prefer to work especially with outcasts, with the most difficult delinquents of the slums, the oppressed lepers of society. But it shows as well in those with a mission, those who oppose materialism and corruption, the anti-pharisees, reformers, suffering servants, betrayed martyrs, teachers of love—in short, in almost anyone in our work who is identified with his youthful spirit, because the image of Christ provides perfect example of the divine young man.

But other images and aspects of my psyche can affect my work: the need for fame and power, so that I tend to see mainly the important people in the community and I become what was once called a "society doctor"; or the need for scientific pursuit, so that I become fascinated with the case, the dreams and the symptoms, forgetting the person who is the case, these dreams and symptoms.

The other person in a therapeutic encounter can serve any of these needs. His therapy therefore begins with my therapy, my becoming conscious of the various archetypal images which play through me and force the other into a role he may not be meant to play. For if I am a father, he must become a child; if I am a healer, he must be ill; and if I am enlightened, he must be benighted and astray. These images are part of the set, the scenic background into which, as on to a stage, the other person makes his entry. Clearly, it is not an open situation; nor can it be open in the sense of a vacuum, an absence of archetypal influences. My needs and the style in which I work cannot be purified out by means of a pseudo-openness and impersonal detachment. The less I am aware of my personal needs and how they filter the forces playing through me, the more the archetypal aspects appear directly and impersonally. Counseling is then suddenly plunged into subhuman depths and the demands become inhuman from both parties. No one can control the psyche and keep these forces out, but one can know something of them beforehand and hold to the human side of the line by admitting from the beginning the needs of one's own personal equation. This may mean at times admitting these needs to the other person, which helps to keep to the human side.

Besides influences coming mainly from the background, from the unconscious scene or set, there is another influence coming directly through consciousness. I want to make something of this encounter. I want to help, to do what I can, to get to know, to try to understand. I want to have the other open as best he can. I want to give him something. Yet wanting, getting, doing, trying and giving are all forcefully active. Consciousness, as centered in the ego, as an instrument of will, is a highly active power. Ego-consciousness would extend its realm. It intends to bring under its subjugation whatever free-flowing libido is not bound by the rules of its reason. Owing to its expansiveness and its hunger to subdue and dominate the irrational, it has been classically imaged as a lion and as the sun or a king. The very act of consciousness is as the phenomenologists say an intentional act. We are organizing the field before us, giving it structure, making meanings. We intend something. Even at our best and noblest we want to achieve something, not lose the hour and waste the day. There is somewhere to get—to improvement, to clarity, to health, or to God, no matter what the path. Yet just this getting is the first paradoxical block in the work. As we try, we prevent. The parable from Zen archery says: the more one aims, the farther from the target. It is as if the first step in the encounter were the overcoming of my ego-consciousness, an eclipse of the sun, even if it is for this same sun that I have been consulted.

A solution which keeps the intentionality of consciousness yet foregoes its active thrust has been called the art of listening. This art has perhaps fallen into decline along with that of conversation. Probably conversation as an art depends first upon the art of listening. How to listen? To what to listen? When not to listen? Listening to oneself while listening to the other. Hearing but not listening. Speaking only when the other is listening.

Listening is perhaps less a problem for theologians and ministers since it is akin to meditation and prayer. Prayer has been described as an active silence in which one listens acutely for the still small voice, as if prayer were not asking and getting through to God, but becoming so composed that He might come through to me.

Long before there was psychology or counseling in the modern sense, before we were instructed to "listen with the third ear," there was contemplative listening, a passive awareness of what is before one. The natural scientist or the painter is devoted to the object before him. He gives himself to it, letting it enter into him. He listens, losing his intense subjectivity in the object, becoming himself an object among objects without the willed intention of ego-consciousness, objectively, registering what is going on. In order to feel the nature of listening we must make a difference between the ego and consciousness. As long as the ego is identified with consciousness, as long as all the light of the psyche is gathered together and aimed, it will be experienced by anyone on whom it is turned as an active, even perhaps aggressive, force. He will then turn on his own light. The two lights will search each other out, brightness against brightness, a dazzle of power. This sort of encounter is familiar enough. But the ego can be separated from consciousness, as the eye and hand are organs different from the ear, each having its own function and adding its own contribution to consciousness. The ear discriminates among the given. A receptive consciousness can grow by means of the organ of hearing just as an active consciousness develops through the hand. The ear can get nowhere, make nothing, do no one harm. We receive the other as if he were music, listening to the rhythm and cadence of his tale, its thematic repetitions, and the disharmonies. Here we become mythologists of the psyche, that is, students of the tales of the soul, as mythology originally means "storytelling." If the soul is a chord only the ear can reveal it. The ear is the feminine part of the head; it is consciousness offering maximum attention with a minimum of intention. We receive another through the ear, through the feminine part of ourselves, conceiving and gestating a new solution to his problem only after we have been fully penetrated by it, felt its impact, and let it settle in silence.

Such listening, allowing the other to come through in his own way, this letting rather than trying, can lead to what is called in Jungian analysis psychic infection. This is another of the risks in an encounter. Where there is real connection and the gates are open, two psyches flow together. One speaks of a "meeting of souls." At this moment, by taking the other one as oneself, one loses the sense of who is who, what is yours and what is mine. It can become *folie à deux*. For a good reason we hold to the ego; its directed intensity is the first defense against such infection, for the ego keeps us independently intact, uncontaminated, our lenses clean. Yet the ego for all its value as a guard is not the therapist. Healing comes from our unguarded side, from where we are foolish and vulnerable. This is expressed by the idea of the wounded healer, who heals through his own wounds—or needs or call. A wound is an opening in the walls, a passage through which we may become infected and also through which we affect others. The arrows of love both wound and heal and are calls. Compassion does not flow from the ego. Yet open wounds if they are not attended to daily can take on alien infections and then disease a whole personality. Again, I will be forced to pay attention to my own sufferings and needs, if I am to be of service to anyone else.

Of all the obstacles which come in the way of any encounter, curiosity deserves special notice. I do not mean the morbid or perverted curiosity of which we each have our share as part of the evil or original sin without which it is inconceivable that we exist at all. Curiosity is not only sublimated scoptophilia or voyeurism, the lubricity of vicarious living through another's dirt and thrills. Anyone engaged in work involving privacy has to come to terms with this side of his nature. Curiosity can indeed be nothing more than a nose for gossip arising from unlived life and life lived through others.

But curiosity is also a deeper failing. To St. Bernard of Clairvaux, whose *Nosce Te ipsum* describes the spiritual discipline of self-knowledge, the primary step off the path in the wrong direction was not pride, not sloth, not lust—but *curiositas*. St. Bernard speaks mainly of its destructiveness in regard to oneself, of the harm the curious mind can have upon peace of soul and spiritual enlightenment. The ego, with its light, attempts to ferret out causes in hidden recesses of the personality, searches for detailed childhood memories, promotes sweet sessions of silent introspection. We are curious to know who we are and how we got this way, whereas the religious attitude would recognize from the first that we are God's creatures and we are what we are owing to His purpose working in the soul rather than to accidents of upbringing and circumstance. Interpreted in terms of depth psychology, St. Bernard's caution means allowing the unconscious to come in its own way at its own time without trying to piece together in a curious fashion a case history as an explanation in answer to the question "why."

So, too, *vis-à-vis* the person in the other chair, curiosity awakens curiosity in the other. He then begins to look at himself as an object, to judge himself good or bad, to find faults and place blame for these faults, to develop more super-ego and ego at the expense of simple awareness, to see himself as a case with a label from the textbook, to consider himself as a problem rather than to feel himself as a soul.

In practical work, curiosity manifests itself in questions. I am asked: "Do other people have dreams like this?" Or a person reads Klein, Horney, Fromm, in order to find out how "other schools" would treat the same problem. This is often called "intellectualization," but it is rather a problem of feeling. Curiosity springs from feelings of doubt and uncertainty; one needs to find others to confirm experience rather than having faith in oneself. Curiosity destroys trust in the analyst or counselor by continual comparisons, by attempts to get outside the situation and judge it, decide about it, from a so-called objective point of view. The objective point of view is a place on the hillside where one is out of the feeling-maelstrom. But there is as much objectivity plunged into the center of the turning wheel as there is far and high above looking down.

Curiosity not only hounds and ferrets; it badgers and hangs on like a bulldog. Once some secrets have come out and been confessed they do not need to be referred to again and again, built into cornerstones for a psychopathology. The aim of confession is lustration; what is washed away is gone, carried off by the river to a far sea. The unconscious can absorb our sins. It lets them rest, giving the feeling of self-forgiveness. Curiosity wants to find out what the sins are doing now: are they really gone? isn't there something else? In this manner curiosity does not let a complex wither. Instead, it feeds the complex, bringing to it new possibilities, increasing guilt. Nothing can lead an encounter more astray—and under the illusion of progressive therapeutic discoveries—than when a person gripped by the urge scrupulously to confess falls into the hands of a counselor of insatiable curiosity. Curiosity is negative introversion, narrowly introspective rather than openly contemplative. Thus *The Cloud of Unknowing* considers curiosity a part of activity and not fitting to the contemplative life—that is, the listener's attitude. Also that great director of souls, Fenelon (1651-1715), in his *Spiritual Letters*, declares that curiosity is overactivity. He describes how the conversation between two people in two chairs takes place. In brief, he finds it necessary that one turn to someone from time to time (a confessor, a counselor, an analyst). And he says,

> It is not necessary that such a person has arrived, or has better behaviour than you. It suffices that you converse in all simplicity with some persons well removed from all intellectualization and all curiosity. (*Letters* ¶ 156.)

That "some person," the counselor, according to Fenelon, need not have specially good behavior, need not be a moral paragon or the exemplary man, but he would have stilled his curious and inquiring mind.

Modern forms of curiosity show themselves very well in analysis, especially where much attention is paid to psychodynamics. Analysis of this sort, whether concerned with early childhood, or with transference reactions, goes by way of prying and inquiring, as if the depths of the soul could only be penetrated through curiosity about them. Then we find the endless tracing of associations, the figurings-out of mechanisms, and diagnoses which lead to the amateur use of clinical language as a popular pastime (the epithets "neurotic," "paranoid," "manic"). Who can figure out another person? Who can figure out himself? Who can add one cubit to his stature with worrying introspection? God alone may know us, but this knowledge surely is not the result of His having figured us out, solved us like a puzzle. Especially misleading is the notion that if we assiduously gather the details of a case we can piece together the mystery of a person. Details of life's accidents, unless they be representatively symbolic, are never essential to the soul. They form only its collective clutter and peripheral trivia and not its individual substance. The person who comes to counseling comes to be freed from the oppression with accidents, to find truth by stepping clean out of banalities which he himself recognizes as such but is obsessively trapped within. The task at this point is to leap qualitatively into the unknown, rather than to find out more by inquiring into the bits and pieces for the sake of finding a pattern. How much time old people give to their reflections and memoirs and how little pattern they can discover after all their long lives! The longer and better one knows another, as in a deep analysis extending through the years, the less one can say for sure about the true root of the trouble, since the true root is always the person himself and the person is neither a disease nor a problem, but a fundamentally insoluble mystery.

Curiosity in psychology today shows itself also in psychological testing. There are now thousands of standardized and copyrighted psychological tests, and there are professional people who make their living by the use of these tests. Curiosity for them has become a refined technique and a good source of income. Testing is a respected professional work; there are Ph.D.'s in curiosity. Tests attempt to treat the psyche or soul as a puzzle that can be solved, taken apart, put together, counted, labeled, known. Tests make us curious about ourselves, our traits and tendencies. Besides making us competitive, they take us outside ourselves as experiencing subjects, splitting us apart into an observer and an object. A question calls for an answer; the subject demands an object. Curiosity does not unite. It raises doubts and gnaws at self-confidence, my faith in myself. Where I am being tested by someone else, that table and pad and questions are between us. There is no connection, no encounter.

Pastoral counseling is not necessarily spared the effects of test psychology, for when a minister interviews someone with an attitude borrowed from this sort of psychology, when he asks for school and work and sexual data, when he attempts to tabulate results or score another for achievements, his little psychological knowledge has become a dangerous thing.

Psychodynamic analysis and test psychology are only two of the ways curiosity has affected our work today. There is another: behavior analysis or the microanalysis of communication. This method records, and even films or views through one-way mirrors, a meeting between two people in order to analyze it, to find out what goes on and what goes wrong. Every gesture, posture, inflection, pause, interruption, is studied for the clues it reveals. A great deal of the unconscious can be made conscious in this manner. Someone watching me for my foibles and listening to the way I speak rather than to what I am saying will pick up much evidence for habits that are unconscious to me and be able to tell me much about the way in which I express anxiety and communicate uncertainty to another person. We do not always know that we tend to hold our thumbs clenched inside our fists, or frown worriedly, or sit slumped disinterestedly.

All these current methods of getting to know the other person, of using curiosity through psychodynamic analyses, projective tests, or tape recordings, have recently been pushed on us who are engaged in human problems as aids to our work. But does knowledge obtained at the expense of splitting observer and observed even further apart, and splitting the individual within himself from himself, aid in the care or cure of souls? And what of this knowledge can be realized and integrated by the developing personality whose suffering is part of his growth? We might ask why these methods have appeared and whether they are not rather substitutions for the immediate and vulnerable human connection. It is as if we had become so isolated and trapped in our ego defenses that an entire psychological spy apparatus had to be invented for communication between the keeps of our interior castles. The city and nation divided against itself is a symbol of our times, and where there is no human connection through the wall between East and West or North and South, then the curiosity systems of the spies proliferate. "Watch yourself," "Look out now," become the words, rather than "Listen, and give ear. . . ."

All methods of curiosity of mind block the meeting of minds. Where they would get through defenses, they only succeeded in causing alarms that tighten security. Spontaneity and the free-told tale gushed forth helter-skelter are stopped. One's account of oneself becomes cold mutton, for all emotion is being kept in reserve lest one give oneself away.

In other words, the first block to knowing another is wanting to know another. Here is where my needs come to my aid. If my need to be an analyst or a counselor is genuinely rooted in my being as a call to be what I am, part of my own realization of personality, I can express that need to fulfill myself without pressing forward professionally into the domain of the other. My questions then will not arise from curiosity, nor will my knowledge derive from detached observation. Rather, my questions are part of my own quest to explore human nature, myself included. Questions of this sort have no answers; but they do evoke responses. And these responses are a spontaneous movement on the part of both toward the essence of the matter at hand. Curiosity about fact and detail gives way before the open contemplation of what is, just as it comes. By abandoning techniques of interrogation, the questioner frees the answerer from being identified with his answers, trapped into his case history, his accidental life, guilty for what he has said. The interview, redeemed from the inquisitional model, transforms into an encounter.

"Prudens quaestio dimidium scientiae." The imprudent question arising from curiosity not only infringes upon secrecy and a person's inner worth and world. It also fractures distance. All animals have a natural sense of distance. When birds sit on a telegraph wire, or gulls on the railing of a pier, they sit a certain distance from each other. When a stray cat crouches on a wall as I pass, it stays fixed watching until I come to a certain invisible line, then it flashes off. Circus animals are trained through the manipulation of psychic distance. The lions are let into the arena one by one and sit each on his stool, not too near one another. If the trainer moves in too closely with his whip or chair, which are extensions of himself, he sets off the flight-or-fight reaction in the animal. It must either flee from its position or slap out with a paw and snarl. A sign of taming an animal is the gradual diminishing of its natural distance. Trust is shown by the animal when it lets another animal or trainer overcome its "critical distance" and move in closer and closer without the instinctual reaction of flight-or-fight.

In the encounter between humans these same animal patterns operate. Through the course of civilization we have been able to separate physical distance from psychological distance. We can stand in a crowded elevator or be examined naked by a physician without feeling that our psychological distance is invaded. We have psychological defenses at our service behind which we can protect ourselves. But in an encounter between two people, deep reactions of natural distance nevertheless still do affect the connection. The problem of distance, of how near to get, comes into every meeting. Some people about whom the word hysteria is used seem to come too close too soon. Others called schizoid seem remote even as they describe their feelings. In a situation where one moves in too quickly with tests or interviews or requests for confession, natural distance may easily be fractured, releasing the flight-or-fight reaction. After one interview, the person never comes back. Unable to fight you, he has taken flight.

Each person has his own space; moreover, one cannot expect a complete display of a basic problem until there is space for it. A basic problem is a painful confusion. It seems to fill a person's whole life, being of enormous weight, trailing off-shoots and attachments throughout his growth. It has neither beginning nor end, and it cannot be dealt with unless a great deal of psychic space has been allowed it. It is, as well, kept in a psychological space of its own characterized by an atmospheric tension, a mood of depression or nervousness, of bitterness or longing. No one can take up a basic problem except by going into and living within this atmosphere in which the problem is kept.

If someone has distance to his problems and shows this by describing them clearly, using diagnostic categories and reporting freely traumatic incidents, it is a rule of thumb that an essential part, the very key to it all, has been omitted. Since problems in psychology are not something people have but something people are, it is not uncommon to work with people for many weeks—even as long as a year—before getting close to what the real matter is, near to the reason why the person has come to therapy at all.

When the great circus cats enter the cage, they follow each other according to feelings of sympathy and antipathy. Some lions will not follow others, some will side with others in a struggle, some will identify with the strongest, or with the trainer. The relevance of this in group work is evident. In all cases the lion-tamer occupies the cage first; it is his space and the lions recognize this. So, too, the analyst or counselor is in his office first, it is his room, his space. The tiger occupies his new cage at a zoo by urinating in all its corners. He makes his mark at the boundaries of his existential space. The analyst or counselor puts his little objects around, hangs his tokens on the walls, paints the woodwork his favorite color.

In receiving a person into my room, the animal pattern of the cage is just below the surface. The bush is a world of territories patterned according to scents, crisscrossed by tracks, organized in hierarchies. There can only be room within my office for another if I make room, if I cease to occupy enough space so that the other can come in, not dissolved before my power and authority, but encased in his own atmosphere. For the other person to open and talk requires a withdrawal of the counselor. I must withdraw to make room for the other. To call this client-centered therapy is not enough, for as long as he is the client and it is my room, he is never the center, and his transference projections upon the therapist keep him certain of his inferiority. This withdrawal, rather than going-out-to-meet the other, is an intense act of concentration, a model for which can be found in the Jewish mystical doctrine of *Tsimtsum*. God as omnipresent and omnipotent was everywhere. He filled the universe with His Being. How then could the creation come about? Not through emanation, God issuing forth from Himself, for there would be no space, and if there were space it would imply an imperfection of God, a place empty, where He was not. Therefore, God had to create by withdrawal; He created the not-Him, the other, by self-contraction, self-concentration. From this doctrine many mystical speculations arose concerning the hidden splendor of God, and its parallels for mystical man, who through intensification, withdrawal, and exile from the outer world aids the creation. On the human level, withdrawal of myself aids the other to come into being.

St. John of the Cross states the paradox of distance simply as *"sin arrimo y con arrimo"*: without approaching, approaching.

Where the analyst only exceptionally meets with his analysand outside of his consulting room, and the physician makes house calls ever more rarely, the minister has the unique opportunity of entering the home and performing his pastoral function within the natural habitat of his charge. The discussions which take place about "visits" of the minister, whether he may telephone a member of the congregation if he is worried about him, whether he ought to call on a woman when her husband is at work and she is alone, whether the children should be allowed in or not—in short, the entire question of managing the spatial problem of the human connection, may better be seen as one of attitude rather than as one of technique. Under the influence of psychotherapy and the medical model of the analyst, ministers tend more and more to see their troubled parishioners in their studies ("dens," "lairs," "retreats"). This only cuts the ministers off further from their charges, turning parishioners indeed into patients, owing to the anxiety of the minister about handling the human connection on the spot, where the action is. The minister has a unique opportunity of entering the home, the family itself, where the soul goes through its torments. The tradition of pastoral care shows that the minister not only may make visits, he must make them. The shepherd looks after his flock; his dog follows up strays, has an ear cocked for trouble, and puts its nose in everywhere. This is possible if the shepherd understands distance and does not feel reduced and subdued entering the space of the other.

Keeping distance touches on the nature of secrecy and the respect which secrets demand.[1] The soul not only has secrets but is itself a secret, or, to put it another way, the flight-or-fight reaction in the human protects his most vital psychological truth. His soul is at stake just as the animal feels his life threatened. Of course, secrets wrongly kept act as poisons and the psyche wants to be purged of them through confession. But not all secret life is pathological, nor all shame and shyness due to sins. Secrets shared build trust and trust

[1] The reader might refer to C. G. Jung's illuminating paragraphs on secrecy in his autobiography *Memories Dreams Reflections* (New York, 1963), p. 315f., and also to "Medical Secrecy and Analytical Mystery," the last chapter of my *Suicide and the Soul* (New York, 1965).

tames the flight-or-fight problem of distance. No wonder that there is no such thing as short psychotherapy where the soul is fully involved.

Distance is very often confused with coldness, just as closeness and nearness with warmth. We all do so want to be warm, loving, and open people! The reproach of coldness is one of the most difficult to take—and it is a very common one. Yet often it is not that the counselor or therapist is cold, but that he keeps his distance, keeps contained within himself. This has several effects on the other person. Primarily it constellates the other person as "other," as different, separate, with its painfulness of being himself, alone. If the other is of the opposite sex, my distance emphasizes the difference between us, which is symbolized at its most basic as sexual polarity. Distance creates us into man and woman; fusion makes us both or neither. So, of course, the polarity is experienced as attraction or repulsion and we are caught by the phenomena of transference. Emotion appears and deep counseling begins. Secondly, my distance gives the other person a chance to come out, to make a bridge, to bring into play his own extraverted feeling and emotion, even if only at the wordless level of weeping. Thirdly, it constellates dignity and respect for the problems. Nothing gives the soul more chance than quiet; it cannot be heard above noise. This may sound grave and pious, and any attitude when put on as medical coat or clerical collar or analytical beard can be misused. But above all we do not want to rouse fear, and there is always tremendous fear—flight-or-fight—where the soul is concerned. The danger of its loss, of damage to it, of its being misled, falsely advised, judged, damned—all are present during the therapeutic encounter. And it is mainly in fear and from fear that we are sought out. The fear may be projected upon us so that we represent the unconscious as threat and enemy. Since only "perfect love casts out fear," fear must at least be banned from the setting until love can equal its power. As long as fear is present, the space of counseling may best be regarded as a temple preserve or *temenos,* a permissive sanctuary giving refuge from fear. Active love cannot redeem from fear, whereas stillness, coolness, darkness, and patience may provide the cave in which to hide until the night is over. First shelter, only later the fire which warms and gives light. Active love cannot redeem from fear since the deepest core of fear—as religious and psychological observers concur—is the fear of love itself. Love's imperfections so long suffered from childhood onward have led to this fear in which love lies hidden, a complex of excruciating sensitivity. To touch this complex even with loving counseling can be therapeutic only when fear abates and only when issuing from one whose love is "perfect"—however that may be understood. Only such love casts out fear, but such love is none of our doing, not of our making. It is beyond the direct touch of counseling which lies in its shadow; as if every human encounter lay under the wing of the dove, as if the shadow of all counseling is the darkness of love.

Theologians take every opportunity to affirm that God is Love. Analysts spend much of their writing time on aspects of love in family, in sexuality, in transference. Why must we do so much preaching and writing about love since we are always immersed in it in one form or another? Why is it so necessary to state that the greatest of the virtues is love and why so necessary to prove that neuroses are imperfections and vicissitudes of love? If love is so ontologically fundamental for theology and psychology why can we not just let it be? Why does it not just happen and why are we not aware of its utter uncomplicated simplicity as we are of other ontological fundamentals which just happen? If love is the essence of man and of God, from whence the impediments? Why its darkness? Why the terrible troubles of love?

Questions of this sort have no answer; nevertheless, analytical experience does tell us something about why loving is so difficult and why distance and secrecy and coolness all may be necessary. They give protection against love—and love wounds. The myths say love is experienced through the arrow of Eros. In Plato, it is a divine frenzy, a *mania*. Jesus' love led to the cross.

The human encounter is difficult because it leads to that wounding experience, that *mania*, that exhaustion of the only-human. At a distance, separated by interview techniques, we are less easily reached and touched; the arrows may fall short. Curiosity excludes the heart. In a group, we are not so soon singled out, chosen, encountered. Alone, there are no eyes to meet mine. But in the human encounter of two people in two chairs meeting each other we have a primary situation of loving. Alone in a room, face to face, in secrecy, the soul laid bare, the future at stake—does this not constellate the archetypal experience of human love? We come no further in our understanding by pejoratively naming the experience "projection" or denigrating it as "transference." Two people committed to each other and to the course of their involvement in the sufferings of the psyche are at once played through by the archetypal force of love. This is yet stronger where they together hope through their encounters to create a new life as a result of their union. We do well to bear this reality in mind from the beginning as a given of the situation, else it may hit from behind and we may fall in it; we may fall in love, regardless of the sexes, the ages, the conditions. Then it is well to remember the *Song of Songs*: "I adjure you that ye stir not up nor awaken love until it please."

Love does not please until we can somehow cope with it, and we cannot cope with it as long as it is an affect rather than a state of being. Love as a state of being, as Tillich describes it, belongs perhaps to the province of theology. In analysis, we encounter love usually as an affect, an emotional tohubohu. And in counseling love resembles more the affect

35

of analysis than the state of being taught by Paul, Nygren, and Tillich in theological school.

The opposites of desire and inwardness, of action and being, are reflected by two opposing traditions of loving which for simplicity's sake can be called Oriental and Western. Holding to the depth and inwardness of love alone is quietistic. Somehow it is inhuman; it negates the living reality of the object of longing by feeding him or her as an image into love as a state of being to be buried there within. On the other hand, Western charity with its reaching out in contact, its programs of Christ in action and the Church in service of the community, its movement and mission, soon empties the well, a vain gesture beating the air. If depth without action is inhuman and action without depth folly, then the solution to the split between these two ancient notions of love—as desire or as state of being—may depend on the individual analyst or counselor: to what extent he is able to connect within himself his impulse to extraverted action with his introverted depths. These two opposing movements form the individual cross of love, psychologically seen. For the sake of finding the center, one or the other direction may have to be sacrificed for a time. I may be able to come to my depths of loving solely through following the impulse to action, living love to the fullest as an affect, forsaking all that I have learned that such love is not the real thing, only a *mania* and a disorder. Or I may have to renounce a powerful involvement in order to take love back into myself, even though I know this withdrawal betrays personal commitment.

In general, our danger in counseling and in analysis is that of having too short an inward axis to bear the range of our extensive involvements. Indeed, I may love to the uttermost outwardly, but should the vertical connection to the ground of being within myself, to my love of myself, toward myself, by myself, not yet be formed, I will have stirred up a love that cannot please. All the issues we have discussed so far turn on this point: the human encounter depends on an inner connection. To be in touch with you I need to be in touch within.

If I am not connected within myself and you come along and throw a bridge over the distance between us, it may make me rush across through the power of attraction (magnified by the lack of inner ground) to fall into your arms and lose my identity; or I may panic at your invasion. The human connection is an extraverted encounter to be sure, and the communication between people unites through interchange, interview, interpersonal relations. But there is as well the intrapersonal relation, the vertical connection downward within each individual. If I have established this axis, I am present with my feeling, listening, open to myself within myself to whatever comes, anchored, rooted, a fixed and turning pivot which no faery lights from far can fetch away. From the outside this may seem withdrawn, distant, uncurious, closed, and cold; yet this may be only the counter-pull to the horizontal attraction of the encounter. Besides, as I withdraw downward, more space is allowed you to express yourself.

Moreover, two people each inwardly connected are communing with each other as well. Two people may be in the same psychological place, constellated by the same state of soul, in communion without demonstratively sharing. Communion is not only communication. The inner connection is the contact two can have with each other from within, from below; for if I am connected to this moment just now as it is I am also open and connected to you. The ground of being in the depths is not just my own personal ground; it is the universal support of each, to which each finds access through an inner connection. We meet one another as well through reflecting the collective unconscious as we do through expressing ourselves in personal communications. Healing takes place in the same way, depending not so much upon my effect on you or your effect on me, but upon the effect of critical moments, archetypal events, welling up from within and re-

37

flected in our meeting. In each such moment some need of the common human soul is being expressed, and my needs and your needs are being reflected and met without a busy interchange on the personal level. Thus crises are healing just because they take one below personal communications and commiserations into the archetypally signal event. Astonishingly one finds oneself engaged in a Biblical parallel—conniving for a birthright, thrown into a pit by envious brothers, setting a daughter against her mother; or a whale waits to swallow one in midnight depression, and Rahab and Potiphar's wife come calling. Plunged suddenly to this level of the impersonal and ever-recurring one-time-only moment, the turning point at the crossroad, two people stand together experiencing the event, together attempting its meaning.

As communion of this sort differs from communication, so does intimacy differ from community. The attempt to reestablish the Christian community through groups—for all its achievements, which are not my task to question—perhaps does fail in regard to intimacy. Here analysis still points the way. In intimacy, I am intimate first of all with myself, allowing myself to feel just what I feel, fantasy just what I do in fact fantasy, hear my inner voice true to life. Through my inner connection I can experience shame, misery, and new pleasures, too. I can come to know myself by revealing myself to myself. In an analysis, the intimacy grows between two people less through the horizontal connection than through the parallel vertical connections of each within himself. Each listens as much to the effect of the other within and to these inner reactions as to the other. Each takes the other in. Each meets the other also in his own dreams and fantasies. From this intimacy, this knowledge from within, community can grow, as some analysts expand their analytical relationships into groups and friendships. But the nucleus remains the intimacy developed within the analysis. For the minister to program intimacy, expecting it as a result of sharing and participation in the community, is to presume that the vertical movement is an offshoot of the relationship between people. Forced intimacy, in groups for instance, usually drives into deeper concealment those parts of the soul which can be shared only where two or three come together, not a multitude.

If the human encounter stirs love as an archetypal force, then the counselor will be glad of the barriers which spring naturally between people, for these are spontaneous defenses. They are not made by the ego; they are rather the ways in which the unfolding growth of the psyche protects itself in shyness and secrecy, in distance and coolness, in reserve and dignity, until it has established the vertical pivot within, that human connection which must balance the developing outer connection between humans. Only when this exists, when this access to my love of myself as I am, fills me with faith in myself as I am and hope for myself as I am, can there be an encounter in the numinous sense of the word. Only then is somebody there, somebody with access to his own vitality, through whom reactions sound and blood-feeling responds, all there, without flight-or-fight, or curiosity.

The movement downward and inward shall occupy us particularly in the next chapter, where the reality of the unconscious is the theme. The human encounter, as the first level of counseling work, leads to the inner connection within the counselor and the counseled. The inner connection leads also to the general problem of what is "inside," that is, the nature of the unconscious. The remaining pages shall explore this inner space.

II

INNER LIFE:

THE UNCONSCIOUS

AS EXPERIENCE

THE PLACE that analysis and theology have in common is the soul. But the soul is a "non-place," for neither theology nor dynamic psychotherapy regards it as its main concern. The one studies God and His intentions, the other studies man and his motivations, while the place in between is too often left unoccupied. This vacuum where God and man are traditionally supposed to meet has become the no-man's land where analysts and clergy confront each other.

Already semantic clouds appear: the words "man," "soul," "God" are used by psychologists rather naïvely, without that immense critical apparatus which trained theologians may bring to bear. When I speak of God meeting man in the soul, I refer to the image of God which the psyche has, the God-image as known, as experienced, as felt, intuited, sensed, as represented or formulated by a person. This "God" is primarily an experience, secondarily a concept. This image or experience is not single nor is it the same. It suffers change in the life of any individual and it differs widely among various individuals. The varieties of divine experience can lead to psychological comparisons, which in turn can lead to theological claims that some images are genuine and others are distortions. Sometimes the experience is absent, sometimes it is a conceptual abstraction, sometimes the divine is displaced on to images and experiences which would not usually be considered holy. Frequently—and this is of no small theoretical interest—the God-image and experience is more distorted or displaced when a person is psychologically more disturbed. Therefore to the psychologist it appears that the experience of God, as well as the image of God, continues to reveal itself in and through the soul without any limits, beyond the confines of any dogma. One such image and experience is the collective representation shared by the minds of all of us in our society. This is the God which the Bishop of Woolwich (John Robinson) is not pleased with, the one up there sitting on high, a child's Father Christmas, old Dharma Dad on a cloud, threatened by supersonic booms and space-walkers in shiny armor. But let us put off until later some of the problems raised by John Robinson and *Honest to God*.

Oddly enough, "soul" is a more difficult experience and image to clarify. As a term, it has all but vanished from contemporary psychology; it has an old-fashioned ring, bringing echoes of peasants on the Celtic fringes or reincarnating theosophists. Perhaps it is still kept alive as some vestigial organ by village vicars and by seminary discussions of patristic philosophy. But it barely enters popular songs—who longs with heart and soul? Who puts his whole soul into anything? What girl has "soulful" eyes, what man a "great soul," what woman is a "good old soul"? "Soul" is the last four-letter word left that is unmentionable among the "in."

Beginning on page 43 and ending on page 47 of my *Suicide and the Soul,* there is an amplification of what I take "soul" to mean. It may be helpful to repeat a statement or two as orientation:

> The first thing that the patient wants from an analyst is to make him aware of his suffering and to draw the analyst into his world of experience. Experience and suffering are terms long associated with soul. "Soul," however, is not a scientific term, and it appears very rarely in psychology today . . . . The terms "psyche" and "soul" can be used interchangeably, although there is a tendency to escape the ambiguity of the word "soul" by recourse to the more biological, more modern "psyche." "Psyche" is used more as a natural concomitant to physical life, perhaps reducible to it. "Soul," on the other hand, has metaphysical and romantic overtones. It shares frontiers with religion. . . .
>
> Exploration of the word shows that we are not dealing with something that can be defined; and therefore, "soul" is really not a concept, but a symbol. Symbols, as we know, are not completely within our control, so that we are not able to use the word in an unambiguous way, even though we take it to refer to that unknown human factor which makes meaning possible, which turns events into experiences, and which is communicated in love. The soul is a deliberately ambiguous concept resisting all definition in the same manner as do all ultimate symbols . . . .

I would now add one more qualifying attribute to soul: it "makes meaning possible, turns events into experiences, is communicated in love—*and has a religious concern.*"

I hope to show as we go on how depth analysis leads to the soul and that this in turn inevitably involves analysis in religion and even in theology, while at the same time living religion, experienced religion, originates in the human psyche and is as such a psychological phenomenon.

Anthropologists describe a condition among "primitive" peoples called "loss of soul." In this condition a man is out of himself, unable to find either the outer connection between humans or the inner connection to himself. He is unable to take part in his society, its rituals, and traditions. They are dead to him, he to them. His connection to family, totem, nature, is gone. Until he regains his soul he is not a true human. He is "not there." It is as if he had never been initiated, been given a name, come into real being. His soul may not only be lost; it may also be possessed, bewitched, ill, transposed into an object, animal, place, or another person. Without this soul, he has lost the sense of belonging and the sense of being in communion with the powers and the gods. They no longer reach him; he cannot pray, nor sacrifice, nor dance. His personal myth and his connection to the larger myth of his people, as *raison d'etre*, is lost. Yet he is not sick with disease, nor is he out of his mind. He has simply lost his soul. He may even die. We become lonely. Other relevant parallels with ourselves today need not be spelled out.

One day in Burghölzli, the famous institute in Zurich where the words "schizophrenia" and "complex" were born, I watched a woman being interviewed. She sat in a wheelchair because she was elderly and feeble. She said that she was dead for she had lost her heart. The psychiatrist asked her to place her hand over her breast to feel her heart beating: it must still be there if she could feel its beat. "That," she said, "is not my real heart." She and the psychiatrist looked at each other. There was nothing more to say. Like the primitive who has lost his soul, she had lost the loving courageous connection to life—and that is the real heart, not the ticker which can as well pulsate isolated in a glass bottle.

This is a different view of reality from the usual one. It is so radically different that it forms part of the syndrome of insanity. But one can have as much understanding for the woman in her psychotic depersonalization as for the view of reality of the man attempting to convince her that her heart was indeed still there. Despite the elaborate and moneyed systems of medical research and the advertisements of the health and recreation industries to prove that the real is the physical and that loss of heart and loss of soul are only in the mind, I believe the "primitive" and the woman in the hospital: we can and do lose our souls. I believe with Jung that each of us is "modern man in search of a soul."

Because the soul is lost—or at least temporarily mislaid or bewildered—ministers have been forced, upon meeting a pastoral problem, to go upstairs to its neighbor, the next closest thing to soul: the mind. So the churches turn to academic and clinical psychology, to psychodynamics and psychopathology and psychiatry, in attempts to understand the mind and its workings. This has led ministers to regard troubles of the soul as mental breakdowns and cure of soul as psychotherapy. But the realm of the mind—perception, memory, mental diseases—is a realm of its own, another flat belonging to another owner who can tell us very little about the person whom the minister really wants to know, the soul.

Perhaps there is justification for the old-fashioned dogmatists who will have nothing to do with these excursions into clinical training and pastoral counseling. They may simply be saying: "The minister does not need the clinic to find the soul or to study its suffering, the *logos* of its *psyche-pathos*. The parish, the world itself, is his clinic. Our concern is not with the mind, its mechanisms and dynamisms, its motivations and repressions and early memories, but with the human soul and its relation with God."

Nevertheless, pastoral training merges more and more with clinical training, as young clergymen studying for advanced degrees fulfill part of their requirements by reading psychoanalysis and by working in psychiatric clinics. This is in keeping with the ideas of the new theology, which I heard the Rev. Harry Williams once define as "that which goes on inside us." From his remarks I understood that what goes on between people in the dining hall or in the bedroom is as much religion as what goes on in Church. Bishop John Robinson affirms this position, saying that statements about God are ultimately statements about personal relationships. This is a threat to the psychologists, since what goes on inside us had been named psychology or physiology, and the problems of personal relationships, dinner table and bedroom, have been the bread and butter of the analyst. For decades, ever since Nietzsche declared God dead and Freud found religion to be an illusion, psychology has been extending its domain at the expense of theology, claiming more and more of the soul as its province. Now, suddenly, in the struggle for the soul, the offensive is with the theologians. Yet the threat is not merely a matter of who has the upper hand.

When the ultimate becomes the inner person, and the transcendent the wholly immanent, then the minister must go into the depths of the psyche. Therefore he is obliged to turn to psychology. The confusion of his parish and of the new theology both point in this direction. But much depends upon the way in which pastoral counselors turn to depth psychology, which is—as the analyst's own training exhibits —necessarily a personal encounter with one's own unconscious and only secondarily clinical work with others or an academic study.

In any event, the proliferation of mental health centers with their competently trained personnel and active programs, their quiet rooms for counseling, their instruction media, group meetings and well-designed pamphlets, which spread psychology with the deadly serious enthusiasm of a new religion (receiving state funds) will not help us find the soul. If the soul is not implied from the beginning it will not appear at the end. No matter how healthy we get mentally, we still need soul. And, in fact, we might well ask: Can anyone have mental health at all unless it be founded upon a sense of soul?

The contemporary loss of soul affects all of us. The clergy is no exception. In fact, the problem of many clergymen today is how to find the inner connection with the calling and how to keep this calling alive. The vertical connection downward and inward to the archetypal root of the vocation seems truncated or twisted. Naturally, the minister looks elsewhere, borrowing and imitating methods that seem to work so well for others. But the task of the counselor is essentially different from that of the analyst, the clincial psychologist, and the academic psychologist. And his tradition goes back to Jesus, who cared for and cured souls in many ways: preaching, wandering, visiting, telling tales, conversing, arguing, touching, praying, sharing, weeping, suffering, dying—in short, by living to the full his own destiny, true to his life. Let the clergy follow the *imitatio christi* rather than imitate psychotherapy. If the *imitatio christi* is neglected it falls into the unconscious and works from behind as an *"identificatio christi."* Then we find the counselor who is consciously pursuing an imitation of medical psychology but who is unconsciously motivated by one or several of the Christ images we spoke of in Chapter I. The parishioner then does not know where he stands, feeling himself both ill and sinful, both rationally diagnosed and irrationally demanded from, before his counselor who is at the same time so scientifically open and yet so dogmatically certain.

The parishioner comes to the minister with another set of expectations than those he brings to the analyst. The minister's task is not medical; he is not there to cure in the modern medical sense. His task is not parental; he is not there to give fatherly love. Nor is his task even spiritual in the sense that he must always know and be an exemplar of perfection and wisdom. But as a shepherd who leads souls to God surely his one central task is devotion to the soul, which begins with

46

care for his own. Only the man who is convinced of its reality can convince others. Only the one grasped by psychic reality can grasp the troubles of the soul that are thrown at his feet. Nothing but this deep conviction in the soul gives the sense of soul, so that the problem of pastoral counseling today begins with the minister himself and his relationship with his own soul.

Many ministers are aware of this. The numbers of ministers and their families who have been in analysis grows, and the pressure on others in the vocation to be analyzed or to "get some psychological help" intensifies. There is in the minister today, as I imagine there always must have been in every man of religion wrestling with his faith, that genuine perplexity of the searcher to keep in touch with his calling. Never was the minister more truly one of his flock than when the lostness of the sheep is equaled by that of the shepherd. Theology, shattered and wasted by a hundred-years crisis of faith, is rediscovering the soul, psychology having taken no small part in this connecting process. All the contemporary problems are also in the churches: alcoholism, adultery, homosexuality, psychopathy, tax-evasion, suicide. Nothing protects the minister any longer from his inward-eating doubts. He finds it hard to hide. But just this shaking of the foundations has forced the individual minister to the courage to be and to the encounter with himself. The real reunion of psychology and religion is neither in dogma nor in ecumenical councils nor in action; it is taking place within the soul of the individual minister struggling with his calling. One cannot but be awed with the earnestness of this struggle, witness to which suggests that something is constellated beyond a personal problem. Something appears to be going on in the soul of the clergy that gives hint of historical importance.

Here depth psychology connects to the new theology. Our concern as analysts is with the soul, man in his myth, his individuation process in its historical plight. Just here is also

47

where the minister himself is. He is today, because of the turmoils in theology and in his own vocational life, in many ways more open than is the psychological specialist fastened by the catechisms of his dogmatic semantics and battened down under the soundproofed hatches of big cities' Harley Streets. The new theology and new morality and new reformation—for all their questionable psychology which we shall discuss further on—at least are new. Unfortunately, the psychology of the unconscious shows some small signs of rigidifying as it enters its eighth decade since its birth in a Vienna consulting room. (The comical old and bearded figure in caricatures today is the analyst, not the clergyman. Because the latter has disappeared from the public eye—except for carrying banners in popular crusades—and has become the "invisible man" as was the negro until so short a time ago, we may expect that the laws of compensation will prevail and that a transfigured appearance of the clergyman is in the making.) The image of the "man of God" is being changed by the images in the cauldron of his individual turmoil. By staying true to the turmoil in his soul, through thick and thin, not only is theology being changed but a new way of caring for the soul is emerging. This is the new pastoral care based on the experience of the counselor within himself. Submitting to the psychological changes being wrought within is a task as heroic as any of the contemporary crusades of the churches in action. The individual task always shakes with uncertainty; its path is through shadows and its rewards come late.

So the problem of finding the soul again burns as perhaps no other issue. The location of God, the meaning of love, the role of the pastoral counselor in the community, and all the rest are derivative issues. He who has lost his soul will be finding God anywhere, up above and down below, in here and out there; he will cling to every straw of love blown past his doorway as he stands waiting for a sign. Without some

sense of soul, there will of course be vast confusions of morality, uncertainties of action, decisions logically sound but not
psychologically valid. Therefore before psychology and religion quarrel over to whom the soul belongs, let us first go
in search of it, together.

From what some theology says, the soul is not in the Sacra-
ments, not in the Liturgy, not in the Ritual. It is not even
to be found in the Churches and Synagogues. They have become community centers catering for almost every need but
that of the soul. The traditional places—so says much influ-
ential contemporary theology—are emptied of all soul; and
even God, declared by Schweitzer, Bultmann, and Barth to be
not really among the existents, has been driven out of the
temples to the very perimeters, his own Lambarene.

Yet as the churches emptied, the clinics filled, and the
depth psychologists—especially Jung—seemed to find soul
and a living God-image in the midst of their work. So theology is now looking in another direction for which there is a
long religious tradition. It is turning within, down to the
"ground of being." If this is the new direction, then the first
place to look is the unconscious, since the phenomenological
place for the unconscious is down and in. This may be the
right track, and others are on to it. Depth psychology, exis-
tentialism, and the mode of the new theology all point downward. The new mysticism is one of descent, as the Rev. Otis
Maxfield has said. It is not a climb up the seven-storied
mountain, to the tops of Carmel or Zion. Or perhaps, as Jung
put it, the way up is the way down and the way down is the
way up.

But let us not make the muddle that it is of little difference
whether the journey is up or down. If we discover the place
of the soul—and the experience of God—to be darkly within
and below, we must reckon with a perilous voyage. The
lower positions (the dark, the down, and the deep) are the
realm of the devil and his horde of demons. The way of

49

descent means the way through the labyrinth, and even theological tradition tells us that the descending path means a confrontation with all things which have been put down through the ages: matter, physis, the female, evil, sin, the lower body, passion. This is of course the classical route of analysis: the return to the repressed. The way of descent may yield an encounter with the "ground of being," but Dante, who also made this journey, found other things as well. Therefore we shall not be able to come to the soul and its experience of God unless we go via the unconscious, which means nothing less than an encounter with the sins and evils, all the turmoil of possibilities that have been kept out of conscious civilization. These are the shadows in counseling. We shall take up the specifics of the descent in the last two chapters.

The unconscious then is the door through which we pass to find the soul. Through it, ordinary events suddenly become experiences thereby taking on soul; through it, meaning becomes vivid again as emotions are stirred. And it is through the unconscious that many people have found a way into love and a way into religion and have gained some small sense of soul. This is confirmed again and again in analytical practice. Yet to look for the soul in the unconscious requires that we first find the unconscious. And since finding means recognizing, we are obliged to go over the simple empirical ground, the very basics, of how we recognize that there is "such a thing" as an unconscious. We shall not establish its existence, nor the existence of the soul either, by argument, by reading, or by any direct proof. We stumble upon it; we stumble upon our own unconscious psyches.

The classical demonstrations of the unconscious are all of the "stumbling" sort. The unconscious is not proved logically. The idea of an unconscious mind has been held to be a logical contradiction; for what is mind if not consciousness? So the proof of the unconscious is experiential; it is a hypothesis, an inference, derived from living experience. Let us review some of the classical demonstrations for the existence of the unconscious. It is worth going over this ground since so much use is made of the word in contemporary writings that at times a reader feels a question is being begged and that in place of ghosts and gods psychologists have invented a hypostasized fiction. That it is not a fiction we shall now see.

Forgetting and *remembering* show us that the mind can lose something and yet not lose it; the mind simply stores it somewhere, and then brings it out again. Beyond what is in sight in the living room, there is an attic and a cellar of accumulated events more or less available, but at least potentially conscious even if not now conscious. *Habit* is another such stumbling proof. We drive the car, smoke a cigarette, handle a knife to cut bread, performing these actions partly consciously, partly unconsciously. How much of habit is unconscious we realize only when we stumble, when the cigarette drops its ash or the knife falters, when we notice what we are doing. *Slips of the tongue,* or what Freud has called the psychopathology of everyday life, further show that we are not alone in ourselves, that the ego personality cannot control everything, that we may to our shame say just the wrong thing or twist a word giving it an entirely different meaning. This is a fear of everyone who must lecture or give a sermon. Suddenly, we stumble into the unconscious.

The *word-association experiment* is another classical proof of the existence of the unconscious. At the beginning of this century, when Jung was a young psychiatrist at Burghölzli, he experimented with word associations, an investigatory method which had been employed in some detail before him by Wundt in Germany. Jung, however, applied the experiments to his patients, thereby stumbling upon some remarkable things about the psyche. He found that when asked to say in as short a time as possible the first word that comes into one's head as a list of a hundred words is read aloud, people stumbled and faltered. Certain words took an over-long number of seconds, other words were perseverated, repeated, and no one could just go through the hundred words without disturbances in association. The focus of attention, the ego control of the subject, was put off; something intervened. On examination of the words which led to this disturbance, Jung found that they seemed to be curiously associated with each other; they formed a complexity of meanings, such as bride, white, fear, Mother, death; and he coined the word "complex" to describe these bundles of feeling-toned ideas which were part of our psychological makeup and which were not fully under the control of consciousness. Through his own independent research, he had experimentally stumbled upon the unconscious and therefore he was one of the earliest to embrace Freud's hypothesis of an unconscious mind.

The complexes can become so dissociated from the ego-personality and even from each other, and they can gather to themselves such strength and form, that they become independent personalities. Then we have another classic demonstration of the unconscious: *multiple personality.* Familiar are the cases of Morton Prince, of the three faces of Eve, and the peculiar splitting of the personality in trance states of mediums. Again, can we not find here the soul disguised in the unconscious? If there are multiple personalities, are we not speaking in traditional language of a multiplicity of souls, or a soul possessed by demons, or split into parts and at war within the breast? The dissociation of complexes and their extreme unconsciousness leads to a belief in spirits, to the experience of parts of oneself projected out there as ghosts or partially real personalities. In this way we may speak of a soul haunted owing to its unconsciousness.

But complexes, as bundles of feeling-toned ideas, can be met without benefit of the association experiment, without lie-detection tests the basis for which was the word-association experiment. We fall over our complexes daily. The unconscious is always immediately at hand. Coming into a room, we catch sight of a man we fear, someone to whom we owe money, a woman we once loved—and our whole habitus, posture, facial expression changes. We may block over a name, blush, or tremble. The voice drops to a whisper or rises nasally. We say something we never meant to say at all. These events happen to us beyond any concious intention. In society one is constantly at the mercy of the unconscious and its complexes, as we strain to impress, attempt to withdraw, make our foolish demands. The complexes govern to a large extent our reactions, especially the compensatory, inadequate reactions.

Further, we need not even be in company to be made aware of the unconscious. We stumble into it every time we are taken by a *mood*. And moods come unbidden, shifting and weaving complexities. A sign of the activation of the unconscious is mood shift and swing. Not only the moment-to-moment flare-ups, fits of pique, waspishness, the tantrums which we allow ourselves in front of our children and wives (and which we do not allow to them), but moods of the unconscious rule the deeper ground swells of rhythm changes, periods of creative inflation, of prolonged sadness and apathy, of boredom, of dullness and blues. And when we try to differentiate the concept of mood and emotion from the concept of the unconscious and again from the concept of the soul, we run into immense difficulties, for ever since antiquity the notion of emotion and the notion of the soul have been and still are intimately connected. Research for the soul's location in the body has always been confounded with the search for the seat of the emotions. Why are emotion and soul so intimately bound up? Mainly because the experience of the soul and the experience of emotion are alike. It is through emotion that we get the exaggerated sense of soul, of honor, of hurt, of anxiety, of our own person. In emotion we get the awareness that we are not alone in ourselves, not in control over all of ourselves, that there is another person, if only an unconscious complex, who also has something—often a great deal—to say about our behavior. So again, the finding of the soul through the unconscious is a stumbling sort of discovery. We fall into emotions, moods, affects, and discover a new dimension which, much as we wish to rid ourselves of, leads us downward into depths of ourselves.

As one penetrates deeper into the essentials of oneself, one feels that personal problems take on a general human dimension and that the essential truths about oneself become universal, quite like the statements of theology. It would appear that deep analysis leads to a strange dark center where it is difficult to differentiate the unconscious from the soul and from the image of God.

It is for this reason, and not owing to wayward theological interests, that analysts become so involved with religious problems. We are not spoiled priests who have missed a calling. The soul is so entangled with the unconscious, and the problems of religion are so vital to the soul, that we are led willy-nilly into statements about God simply from being witnesses to the confused discoveries of Him during an analysis. When Jung claims that the psyche has a natural religious function he is not proselytizing for natural religion, nor for any religious vested interest, even if many would now use Jung to shore up wobbly convictions.

The natural religious function is inherent within the process of analysis itself. The way in which analysis brings change to a person and the evidence for this change (as "cure") is astonishingly similar to patterns of religion. To characterize this process in shortest terms: Analysis begins with inwardness and washing of oneself. This prolonged labyrinthine

54

work often leads to a revelation of truth and a new vision of oneself with changes of attitude expressed through language of renewal, conversion, or rebirth. Finally, this is affirmed in witness and demonstrated in lived life. Therefore the analyst turns to religion for adequate understanding of the phenomena in his own work.

The unconscious also shows itself in *symptoms;* not only in the symptoms of affect, of split personality, or of forgetting and slips of the tongue, not only in the psychological symptoms, but in physical symptoms where there is no ground in the organic system, no mark or trace or logical cause. Even more, there are the symptoms which are organically demonstrable but called psychogenic. These of course are not caused by the conscious personality, not by what we will, but by the unconscious personality.

That these symptoms can lead to discovery of the soul is no longer a remarkable statement. And I do not mean *Reader's Digest* miracles like "How My Headaches Led Me to God." But a prolonged occupation with suffering, with the incarnation of oneself in flesh which is tormented for apparently no reason, to be afflicted like Job in spite of being godly to the best of one's ability, is a humiliating, soul-awakening experience. Symptoms humiliate; they relativize the ego. They bring it down. Cure of symptoms may but restore the ego to its former ruling position. The humiliation of symptoms is one of the ways we grow humble—the traditional mark of the soul. We talk much of humility, but we say little about how it comes about. Humility cannot be turned on, since it is not an ego act. There is however such a thing as positive humiliation, which is not a rejection, not masochistic, not breaking, but which may be as near religious humility as we may ever know.

Because symptoms lead to soul, the cure of symptoms may also cure away soul, get rid of just what is beginning to show, at first tortured and crying for help, comfort, and love, but which is the soul in the neurosis trying to make itself heard, trying to impress the stupid and stubborn mind—that impotent mule which insists on going its unchanging obstinate way. The right reaction to a symptom may as well be a welcoming rather than laments and demands for remedies, for the symptom is the first herald of an awakening psyche which will not tolerate any more abuse. Through the symptom the psyche demands attention. Attention means attending to, tending, a certain tender care of, as well as waiting, pausing, listening. It takes a span of time and a tension of patience. Precisely what each symptom needs is time and tender care and attention. Just this same attitude is what the soul needs in order to be felt and heard. So it is often little wonder that it takes a breakdown, an actual illness, for someone to report the most extraordinary experiences of, for instance, a new sense of time, of patience and waiting, and in the language of religious experience, of coming to the center, coming to oneself, letting go and coming home.

The alchemists had an excellent image for the transformation of suffering and symptom into a value of the soul. A goal of the alchemical process was the pearl of great price. The pearl starts off as a bit of grit, a neurotic symptom or complaint, a bothersome irritant in one's secret inside flesh, which no defensive shell can protect oneself from. This is coated over, worked at day in day out, until the grit one day is a pearl; yet it still must be fished up from the depths and pried loose. Then when the grit is redeemed, it is worn. It must be worn on the warm skin to keep its lustre: the redeemed complex which once caused suffering is exposed to public view as a virtue. The esoteric treasure gained through occult work becomes an exoteric splendor. To get rid of the symptom means to get rid of the chance to gain what may one day be of greatest value, even if at first an unbearable irritant, lowly, and disguised.

But the main way in which we stumble upon the unconscious, that *via regia* as Freud called it, is the *dream*. The dream itself is a symbol; that is, it joins in itself the conscious and the unconscious, bringing together incommensurables and opposites. On the one hand, nature: natural, spontaneous, unwilled, objective psychic contents and processes. On the other hand, mind: words, images, feelings, patterns and structures. It is a senseless order, or a structured disorder. Every night the bridge is thrown up by the unconscious side of the psyche. Every morning for a moment or two while we are still in the dream we are living the symbol, living it in, united in an existential reality, true to life as we are at that moment. This state is hard to maintain. The press of the day pulls the ego away. The conscious pole of the psyche lets go its end of the bridge. We stumble upon our dreams—too often only to kick them aside.

The classical Jungian attitude toward the dream is expressed very well by a term I would borrow from existential analysis. (The existentialists have a way with words and can often give something all analysts have been doing for decades a turn and flourish that effects the thrill of a new discovery.) This term is: to "befriend" the dream. To participate in it, to enter into its imagery and mood, to want to know more about it, to understand, play with, live with, carry, and become familiar with—as one would do with a friend. As I grow familiar with my dreams I grow familiar with my inner world. Who lives in me? What inscapes are mine? What is recurrent and therefore what keeps coming back to reside in me? These are the animals and people, places and concerns, that want me to pay attention to them, to become friendly and familiar with them. They want to be known as a friend would. They want to be cared for and cared about. This familiarity after some time produces in one a sense of at-homeness and at-oneness with an inner family which is nothing else than kinship and community with oneself, a deep level of what can also be called "the blood soul." In other words, the inner connection to the unconscious again leads to a sense of soul, an experience of an inner life, a place where meanings home. As those pieces and parts that before lived unconnected are laced together, are deepened and extended, that habitable dwelling place for religious life about which we spoke at the beginning begins to form itself.

The habit of looking at one's dreams which makes the inner world habitable can begin right within the family. At the breakfast table—as well as talking of what's happening in school today or reading cereal boxes or 'phoning—one can mention a dream image or fragment, in order to allow the unconscious a place within the family, openly, in simplicity. There is no need to interpret a child's dream, or even to explain to everybody why one dreamed this or that. It is enough that the dream is brought into contact with daily existence, that the subjective reality of the dream is admitted, allowed, valued, in the objective world of the family. Interpretations and explanations are too often rationalizations; and why should a child be made to feel ashamed of his dreams, that they are crazy, weird, naughty?

The meanings which grow from the dream cannot be the meanings given by the ego's mind. If that is all there were to it, there would be no growth, there would only be aggrandizement of the ego, a new *pax romana* to which all strange and alien elements must submit. Nowhere is the old saw that "a little learning is a dangerous thing" more appropriate than in regard to dream interpretation. Pastoral counselors seem instinctively to recognize this and say again and again that they "leave dreams alone," as if they were too deep, too difficult, requiring special knowledge and training for interpretation. This is certainly true; yet if the minister is to be a shepherd of souls, how can he ignore this essential voice from the soul, regarding it as a message fit only for Freudians or psychiatrists or Jungian experts to understand? Therefore we must come at the dream in another way, a way which is not for experts alone, a simple practical approach valid at the breakfast table or in parish work.

Let us first realize that we shall not be following the dictum of Freud: where id was there shall be ego. To give a dream the meanings of the rational mind is just to replace the id with ego. Dream interpretation then becomes a kind of dredging up and hauling all the material from one side of the bridge to the other. It is an attitude of wanting from the unconscious, using it to gain information, power, energy, exploiting it for the sake of the ego: make it mine, make it mine. This attitude breaks apart the symbol, which is a joining of the two sides of the psyche. It would translate the dream into something known, a sign or label. (This is a mother substitute; that animal is your sex drive; those hills and valleys are a screen for your childhood home and infantile wishes.) These rationalizing interpretations, by attempting to replace the id with the ego, actually work to drain the unconscious, to reduce its size, to empty it out—all of which are hostile acts. This is not befriending the dream. The dream, when split into irrational content and rationalized meaning, becomes the psyche split. The dream which every morning offers the opportunity for healing our house divided is violated and our wounds stay open, ever-new wet disorder below, ever-new dry order above. Then the unconscious becomes mine enemy which must be worked on or propitiated with analytical techniques, or observed and watched from clever vantage points. But above all it must be depotentiated. Indeed, there are situations which the dreams will reflect as an overgrown swamp, a panic of animals, a sea in storm, a messy kitchen, where rational clarifications and clearheadedness are called for. But what counts most is the relation to the dream stemming in part from the attitude toward the dream.

Friendship wants to keep the connection open and flowing.

The first thing, then, in this non-interpretive approach to the dream is that we give time and patience to it, jumping to no conclusions, fixing it in no solutions. Befriending the dream begins with a plain attempt to listen to the dream, to set down on paper or in a dream diary in its own words just what it says. One takes especial note of the feeling-tone of the dream, the mood upon waking, the emotional reactions of the dreamer in the dream, the delight or fear or surprise. Befriending is the feeling approach to the dream, and so one takes care receiving the dream's feelings, as with a living person with whom we begin a relationship. Then there is to be noted just what the friend is saying, whom he is talking about, and where it all takes place. Dream scenes are usually confined to a few figures, frequently four in all, and therefore it is only this specific message that is being transmitted. If for a few nights mainly men come into my dreams, I know that something is going on with the masculine side of myself, that these figures are all different ways to be a man, that each embodies a special set of characteristics, a complexity representing one salient feature of my own personality. One is particularly ambitious, another is a football hero with a powerful body, a third is indistinct and shifty-eyed. These are all possibilities open to me, parts of myself, as complexes that belong to my nature and influence my behavior. My dreams may elevate me to royal company, have me in airports ready to fly off and away at any moment, find me in impersonal hotel rooms neither here nor there, or take me skimming over ski-slopes, bright and frozen on my metaled tracks. Always the dream is saying: "Look where you are, whom you are with." And the more repetitive the motifs, the places, the people, the more the dream insists that it be attended. Does one ignore a friend?

And the story a friend tells begins somewhere, has a middle, and comes to an end, like all stories and dramas. So I listen to just where the dream begins, for this sets out the opening statement of the concern of this dream, just as the time and place is printed in the theater program: in the morning of a childhood day, at night in the office after everyone has left and only I and the office remain, in my marriage bedroom. I notice as well the way in which the dream builds its involvements to reach a climax, sometimes indicated by the word "suddenly"; and then it ends somewhere, sharply or trailing off, or I awaken.

Although it takes years of familiarity to interpret dreams well since it is truly a specialist's work, a craft as well as an art, it takes no great cleverness or special knowledge to befriend a dream. We can always let this friend ramble on in reverie, spinning the dream along, and then the observer may ramble on too, associating and amplifying, remembering incidents, plays on words, parallels from the Bible and mythology and films. I let it speak and I speak to it—rather than analyze or interpret it. By speaking to the dream, one addresses its mood and images and encourages the dream to go on telling its tale. Here it is necessary to take care throughout that the atmosphere of the dream is respected and the images given validity and dignity, which may be given best by courageous reactions to the dreams, as one must react courageously in a friendship. By encouraging the dream to tell its tale, I give it a chance to present its true message, its mythical theme, and thus get closer to the myths which are operating in me, my real story, the story of my life from within, rather than my case history observed from without. I become my own mythologist, which means originally "teller of tales."

In this way surely the pastoral counselor can begin to listen to dreams as well as to other stories in his work. The dream story is simply the inner aspect of the outer story. As the counselor listens to dreams, his ear for them, like the ear of the storyteller or joke-maker, grows acute. Thus did Joseph and Daniel listen; yet the pastoral counselor may listen better if he foregoes identification with those Biblical dream-analysts, which means not yielding to the temptation of giving authoritative interpretations.

This approach is not amateur psychology, because dreams do not belong to the province of psychology alone. Once they were taken to holy men for interpretation. They belong as much to the man of religion as to the man of psychology, since they are "God's Forgotten Language," as the Rev. John Sanford has called them in a book by that name. Amateur it would be to approach dreams with psychological tools that have not been mastered. Amateur it would be to attempt analytical interpretations without having that devotion to the dream, that responsibility to the unconscious, and that knowledge of objective symbolic material which is the context of dream-formation and is the science of the art. Because the dream has universally been considered an important message, sometimes even from the divine, the interpreter had to be a man set apart in order to handle the powers released through revelation. This has not fundamentally changed despite all serious scientific studies on dreaming; nor will simply befriending the dream resolve its dark language and perplexities. Fate continues to be announced through dreams and sometimes it is doom that is presaged and very little can be unraveled. In spite of all the riddles, it is still less amateur, less dilettantish, to befriend, play with, and fantasy the dream along, since this kind of exploration meets the dream on its own imaginative ground and gives it a chance to reveal itself further. Dreams are part of common humanity and are best approached with common humanity before resorting to special techniques. When the modern minister begins to listen to them, he takes up again one more part of his pastoral task in caring for souls. Caring for souls today means caring for the unconscious. The minister can do this according to his own archetypal background in his own way without having to borrow the clinical methods and psychopathological language of psychology.

If a choice is forced upon the counselor between being himself the amateur with dreams or sending the person to a psychiatrist for "professional help," then let him be bold enough to play. Play may keep the soul alive. The amateur who knows he is playing, is conscious of his ignorance, and trusts the dream to guide him, may well do less harm than that professional who tends to disregard the dream—and the soul—in favor of psychodynamics and drugs. As long as the counselor listens to the dreams he is at least giving ear to the person's soul, even though he may not be able to give in professional language an account of what is going on. The pastoral counselor who feels himself an amateur may take comfort that the dream is by nature an enigma, obscure, oracular, ridiculous, which demands of him who would attempt its meaning a highly unprofessional naïveté. The psychological amateur, or "lover of the psyche," just because of his openly unknowing and humble attitude toward the dream has the opportunity of affirming its value, of giving recognition to its importance regardless of the dream's content. Through his attitude alone he can affirm and recognize this product of the soul, thereby giving value and importance to the soul itself, to its creative, symbolic, awe-inspiring function. Is this not to bless the soul, for what a blessing this is for the psyche and its dream—and for the dreamer—to be affirmed and recognized in this way.

In the startling dreams of terror, of ugly images, and cruelties, we often forget that the unconscious shows the face which we show it. It is like a mirror. If I flee, it pursues. If I am high up, it is an abyss below. If I am too noble, it sends me nasty dreams. And if I turn my back, it attracts and tempts me to turn and look with seductive images. The gulf between consciousness and the unconscious narrows as we are able to feel for it and give to it, as we are able to live with it as a friend. The continued absorption with one's own inner world leads to experiences within that world, in and for that world. These experiences may have little or no connection with outer life, or with ideational life. That is, they may not immediately lead to a new project or idea, or the solving of a marriage or a job problem. They are experiences about events of one's own life. They are in fact a renewal of the capacity to have experiences, to be an experiencing being. Kicks and thrills and the chase for them fade. As the capacity to experience and to love life as it is grows, one needs fewer events because one has more experiences. This growth is growth of soul as I described soul—that is, it makes meaning possible, turns events into experiences, is communicated in love, and has a religious concern.

Religious concern differs from theological or dogmatic concern, for that would be to take up experiences into the already established positions of mental life or outer life, to put them to use and service, to place the soul in the yoke of profession. Rather the religious concern of the psyche comes in the form of spontaneous symbols that have similar representations in religion, such as the cross of opposites, the child in danger, the garden, the mountain, the gate and the guardian, the place of water, the wind, the desert, the grove of sacred trees—images that appear in dreams frequently. Or it arises from the religious motifs such as the importance of love, the battle with evil, the slaying of the dragon, the miraculous turn or cure. And the religious concern comes also in the form of intimations of immortality, eternity, metempsychosis, and questions of death, after-life, and judgment of this soul, what is right for it, where it is, where it will go next. In other words, the religious concern is a spontaneous manifestation of us each when the soul is refound.

Then dogma and theology, too, take on new meaning. For on the one hand, the soul's questions and images are able to be fed by the background of traditional religion. And on the other hand, a sense of reawakened experience brings a freshness to the tradition and gives new meanings to it as the continuation of religion that is continually revealing itself. In other words, revelation stops whenever soul is lost and can no longer give experience and meaning to the basic myths, symbols, forms, and proofs. For psychology, soul comes first—then religion. Yet also for psychology soul does not reach its fullness without realizing its religious concern.

Perhaps we cannot put either psychology or religion "first." The symbolic attitude of psychology arising from the experience of soul leads to a sense of the hidden numinous presence of the divine, while the belief in God leads to a symbolic view of life where the world is filled with significance and "signs." It is as if the soul makes no choice between psychology and religion when they naturally lead into each other.

In this chapter I have rehearsed these classical demonstrations of the unconscious in order to give the experiential, empirical, or phenomenological basis for our right to use the word "unconscious." But I have of course wanted to do more than that. I have hoped to hint that through the unconscious one also stumbles upon soul. Patterns emerge, meanings are discovered; one senses a vital connection to the past, one's own past and that of one's family and people. One's own myth, that of father, hero, follower or master, or healer, shepherd, servant, trickster, merges with the symbolical, mythical images of the whole human race, and through emotion one is moved to experience that things matter, matter very much indeed! And choice counts. And what we do with ourselves, our bodies, our hearts and minds, counts so much that personal worth, dignity, and the importance of my own individuality, my own person, grow from each new bout with the unconscious. In other words, through experiencing the unconscious I gain soul. In particular, through the dreams and through entertaining fantasies and receiving the inner world, it occupies more space in my life and has more weight in my decisions—that is, it gains more substantial reality.

Besides the familiar reality of my mental activity (my introspection, worries, plans, observations, reflections, projects), and the worldly reality of objects, there can grow a third realm, a sort of conscious unconscious. It is rather non-directed, non-ordered, non-object, non-subject, not quite a reality of a concrete kind. Yet it is not quite me; it is something that is happening to me. I do not worry it along as a project or an introspection, nor do I connect it immediately with the outer world of objects. It is a realm for itself, neither object nor subject, yet both. This third reality is a psychic reality, a world of experiences, emotions, fantasies, moods, visions, dreams, dialogues, physical sensations, a large and open space, free and spontaneous, a realm mainly of "meaningness." In these states of soul we can feel connection to nature and to ourselves. We can weep or storm, let lust dance, contend with God, pose the imponderables, and find, without active compulsive meditation, without stern rigors, without LSD and "drug experiences," an inner life come to life. I do not know how better to describe the entrance to this third realm of psychic reality which lies between mind and matter and perhaps governs both in ways we do not yet understand than to borrow from Jung. In practice, he says, the way is often not to analyze but to enter the dream with the patient and dream the myth along.

The conclusion to which we are led is that rediscovery of soul through the unconscious results in both a theological and religious concern. The former appears when we try to formulate this inner religious life with all its contradictory complexities and to relate it to official dogmas about the nature of God; the latter appears in the reawakened presence of inner myth and sense of destiny, the sense that one is somehow meant. To be meant implies a transcendent power that

66

calls, chooses, or means something with one, a power which gives meaning. The inner connection to one's life as a ritual and oneself as a symbol of everyman's common humanity re-mythologizes the course of events, returning numinosity to the mundane.

The connection within provides as well the connecting bridge to the inside of every other man whom we may encounter in counseling; the inner world of dream, of affect and suffering, is all too human, tragically the same for everyone, regardless of educational level, color and geography. The death of a child, jealousy in love, night terrors of the dark, aging, sin, remorse—all images and experiences of my soul are images and experiences of your soul. This field of psychic reality which is immanent to each transcends the individual differences between us, giving us the common language based on our common patterns of experience. Through our unconscious we all connect, experiencing our portion of collectively given images and emotions.

These observations drawn from practice force us to the following conclusion for theology: the movement to de-mythologize religion, to adjust religion to our dry rational outlooks, is patently wrong. From this viewpoint, God is indeed dead. The dead God is the demythologized God, a God disemboweled of emotion, a mental figment without psychic reality. Such religion may be more rationally convincing to the mind—although this too can be doubted. But such religion will not grip the soul, mainly because it leaves out the unconscious where the soul lies. Must we demythologize religion in order to meet modern man? Could we not choose the alternative of involvement with the unconscious thereby reconnecting modern man to his myths? Maybe in this way he will stumble again upon his soul and its naturally religious concern.

III

INNER DARKNESS:

THE UNCONSCIOUS

AS A MORAL PROBLEM

A GREAT difficulty in pastoral work according to the lay imagination is the discrepancy naturally arising between morality as preached and morality as practiced. The minister is supposed to be the paradigm of a split between practice and preaching. The "new morality" of the "new reformation" has brought this conflict into focus and is attempting a new solution.

However, the same shadows are arising in analytical work. Just as one can discuss ethics in the legal, medical, or public service professions, so now as the new analysis separates itself from its psychiatric background, becoming a field of its own, it is beginning to take up the issue of analytical ethics. The moral problems that constellate in the fields dedicated to the service of higher ends are particularly thorny, the split between good and evil particularly peculiar. It seems that as we try to bring light, serve truth, and do good, the opposite side grows with the same intensity. This phenomenon is so independent of our conscious intention, so difficult to face steadily and to cope with, that gradually a dissociation occurs, splitting us apart. At best, we hold the tension and suffer moral pain; at worst, we repress the split and the world suffers it as hypocrisy and betrayal. The split between preaching and practice, consciousness and shadow, hand of wisdom and hand of folly, will hardly be solved by choosing one at the cost of the other. To force practice into the mold of preaching as did the old morality, or to let preaching be led and limited by the facts of practice as would the new morality, only subdues conflict without resolving it. Both preaching and practice are rooted in the same human psyche and have authenticity. Both are realms of action, and perhaps the left hand and the right are obliged to keep their secrets from each other. Rather than choosing one at the expense of the other, there might be another solution. This would be the development of what lies in between, the dark inner space where the heart is, an approach to the cultivation of which is one intention of this chapter.

In the popular mind, those in the pulpit are supposed to be identified with morality, while those in the analytical chair are supposed to be on the side of the id, of unbridled desire, and against morality. One therefore expects the conflicts of religion and psychology to appear not only in the question of who has claim to the soul, but between those who uphold morality and those who would analyze it away. If we look more closely at this, we find the sides sometimes curiously reversed. Today's morality as expounded from some pulpits has a remarkably liberal note with an eighteenth-century openness to life and love. To escape the dead hand of Victorianism, some theological morality in an attempt to move forward seems to have moved backward to the time before Victoria.

When it is held that God is as much in the dining hall as He is in church, is as much in human relationships as He is in the God-man relationship, and when the justification of acts becomes based upon the depth of love between persons, we have given to Augustine's *Love and do what thou wilt,* and his *Only one thing is really enjoined upon the Christian— namely, love,*[1] an astonishingly contemporary twist. Upon love alone all questions of morality are to be decided: "For *nothing else* makes a thing right or wrong."[2] One wonders who now is leading the assault upon the old morality—perhaps the new theology itself?

In today's high-pressure, Mr. Cool world, the boy-Fausts with barbered heads and unlined faces are in the corridors of power. They are appointed to High Government; they disburse the Funds of Foundations; they run the Corporations. Just as the natural science model of thinking affects psychology and theology, so too does this technician-physicist model of man affect psychologist and clergyman. We do not want to be old-fashioned, no longer with it, out. And I believe that the new morality of which Bishop Robinson has written is an attempt to keep in and with it, which may be rationalized as "abreast of the times." The churches want to go with life, true to mid-twentieth-century life, and its ministers do not want to take up moral positions which are split from this life. Therefore this new twentieth-century morality is a theological cloak for the modern trend. *Honest to God* states

> But there is no need to prove that a revolution is required in morals. It has long since broken out; and it is no "reluctant revolution." The wind of change here is a gale. (p. 105)

[1] A. Nygren, *Agape and Eros* (Philadelphia, 1953), p. 454.
[2] J. A. T. Robinson, *Honest to God* (SCM paperback), p. 119.

This is a justification *ex post facto*, a recognition of a revolution and of a new regime not *de jure*, but *de facto*. One sails with the gale rather than being toppled over like the rigid steeple whose old stones are crumbling.

This new morality is supposed to have arisen from the work of Freud. The discoveries of depth psychology are the "scientific" background for the new liberation. But I would like to show that analysis is a moral procedure, requiring a morality, and that this morality of analysis may even point a way out of the dilemma of old morality versus new morality.

The confrontation with the inner world in the ways we have already touched upon may at first be an exciting, inflating experience. A door opens and another world is revealed. Suddenly things long forgotten, or long remembered as insignificant, take on sharp poignancy. Childhood is revisited, and one can go home again. Truths drilled in become truths that flower; and even what one has been preaching to others takes on new sense for oneself. This tends to happen again and again in therapy: in the beginning a person cannot wait for the next dream, the next revelation from the unconscious, or the next analytical hour. At last things are falling into place and there is energy to undertake. The initial contact with the unconscious is a vitalizing experience, as if a fountain long clogged through neglect flows again. And one finds just such energetic images: a stream bed now has water in it, a stagnant pond begins to flow, a herd of animals, a strong horse in a green field, a glacier melts, or engines, dynamos, mechanical turbines, or departure docks for ocean liners, railroad stations, airports, frontiers.

A journey is about to begin; but the excitement and inflation appropriate to the beginning and without which the beginning could hardly be undertaken often turns—just on the other side of the customs barrier, after the ship leaves the harbor or the train the station—this journey turns into a perilous voyage, an adventure through the sea at night or through a desert where one is beset with the full uncanny force of the unknown. Or then the drunkard appears who cannot handle his spirit, or the *nouveau riche,* the big spender, the rude millionaire, the locomotive engineer, or all the inflated leaders of politics and community. The new energy has been taken the wrong way, assimilated by the ego as power and drivenness and outer show.

Freud was the first to describe what is to be encountered when the door is opened into the unconscious and one descends, when one actually confronts, by immersion in, the inner darkness. And it is dark! The unconscious, as we saw in the previous chapter, cannot be conscious; the moon has its dark side, the sun goes down and cannot shine everywhere at once, and even God has two hands. Attention and focus require some things to be out of the field of vision, to remain in the dark. One cannot look both ways at once. It is dark, however, for two reasons: the first because it is necessarily repressed—the world which Freud has so carefully investigated; and secondly, it is dark because it has not yet had time nor place to emerge into the light. This, too, is the inner darkness, the earth or ground of one's new being, the part which is *in potentia,* and which Jungian psychology would cultivate. It is the darkness of the Past and the darkness of the Future. Behind the repressed darkness and the personal shadow—that which has been and is rotting and that which is not yet and is germinating—is the archetypal darkness, the principle of not-being, which has been named and described as the Devil, as Evil, as Original Sin, as Death, as existential Nothingness, as *prima materia.* We shall come back to this soon.

The experience of the inner darkness, as Freud described it, is the vivid confrontation with one's own repressed nature. The beast emerges from his lair where he has long lain sleeping, and a man has night terrors, awakens in a sweat. A corpse or ancestral mummy resurrects. A vast swamp appears behind the Church or behind one's father's house, from which crawls a prehistoric monster with an elongated red phallic neck, and the person who denies his beast wonders how he could ever have dreamt such a thing. A criminal, an idiot child, a piece of feces inside the water spigot staining the fresh water as it flows, an older hardened homosexual, a Nazi —one after another, like a police line-up, they wait for identification and acknowledgment: Yes, this too is mine. "Inasmuch as ye have done it unto one of the least of these my brethren. . . ."

At these moments, when one meets face to face the perverse and amoral creatures who have been inhabiting other parts of the building, the homilies which are usually understood by us in terms of how to be with others become lessons of how to be with ourselves. And suddenly the difficulty of those lessons comes home, for somehow one squirms having to acknowledge the dark truth about oneself. I mean by this not the general idea that "yes, we are all sinners" and born in sin, but that we are specifically responsible for specific actions and for specific character traits which stand contradictory to the light side of ourselves.

This is of course a moral struggle. Remembrance of sin, remorse, and repentance become the living language of an analysis. The woman begins to see what she has been doing out of selfishness all these years to her husband, how she has never really been interested in him. She has only been interested in his interest in her. Or the mother, now a grandmother, catches glimpses through her dreams of her witchery and power tricks with her children. And a man runs across a confidence man in his dreams, a mountebank, a slick salesman, a sociopathic chancer, and he sees how he has slipped out and danced away from his betrayals and years of using other people.

But one can feel a moral failure *vis-à-vis* oneself. This is more difficult and brings with it new moral problems. For one can feel the need to face having wronged others more easily than the need to face having wronged oneself. Collective morality approves of self-sacrifice. We wrong and hate ourselves with full moral sanction of the community. Altruism is said to be the opposite of egoism. Yet, through the unconscious, one discovers that much altruism is sham and compensation if the right sort of egoism has been failed. Rather than living that egoism which is simply faith in hope for, and love of oneself, we keep the egotistic child in us alive, coddling it with childishness, thereby stunting our own potency. To come to full stature might mean putting away all childish things, and this sacrifice not even the community demands. It tolerates all foibles and even perversities rather than have in its midst the grandeur of individuality. Collective morality too often finds little place for the man who has that self-love, that confidence and strength, to come into his kingdom and take possession of it. He is met with envy. As Nietzsche noted, there is ample room in the Christian community for the meek and the weak; the last commandment about covetousness is easy to keep in a collective where only the poor in spirit abound.

When one has a moral obligation to oneself, figures appear in the shadow which represent positive possibilities of one's own nature, potentialities that have not been given a chance. I am guilty not only toward the past, but toward my own potentialities. The shadow often divides between an obedient and dull bourgeois figure who is collectively approved and uncreative, and a bearded beatnik, a rebel or hobo, a fellow with flair but no "pad" to call his own. And again there is a moral problem: for to whom does one give credit at this juncture—the sheriff or the outlaw, the professor or the freshman, the cardinal or the defrocked priest? Who is positive and who is negative? The one-sided light of ego-consciousness implies that darkness means neglect. And it is the neglected elements which appear in the shadow. Where the ego has neglected its own virtues and talents, then these virtues and talents will be incorporated into figures of the dreams who have become social outcasts—that is, cast out by the fixed laws of the way in which we have set up our inner society. Then these potentials must appear as outlaws, misfits, even cripples or lunatics. Healing these, the blind and the lepers, raising the dead, becomes an inner necessity to bring health to the personality.

Symbols of the inner darkness which a person experiences may be seen not only against the personal sins and crimes of an individual's life, but also in the broader view of human development in general. Hercules had to clean the filth of the Augean stables; he had to divert whole rivers of energy to accomplish this impossible labor. He had as well to slay the lion of his own ambition, his own will to power, before he could dirty himself in those stables. Ulysses had to meet the giant of the hungry eye, the single-minded demon of compulsion, before he could proceed on his way. Somewhere there is a monster to be met, a beast to be slain, a drive to be overcome. Somewhere there is an angel to be grappled with before one can ford the river. And when one is alone in a desert, whether the modern one of the suburb or office building or the ancient one of the early Church fathers, all sorts of demons set on one, temptations, seductions, perversions, projections, illusions. There is always a background to every complaint brought, and the more overwhelming and fascinating the complaint, the more sure we can be that there is an archetypal background which is using a symptom for a symbol, and which, if better understood, is not merely a pathological suffering but may become a religious experience.

The cure of the shadow is on the one hand a moral problem, that is, recognition of what we have repressed, how we perform our repressions, how we rationalize and deceive ourselves, what sort of goals we have and what we have hurt, even maimed, in the name of these goals. On the other hand, the cure of the shadow is a problem of love. How far can our love extend to the broken and ruined parts of ourselves, the disgusting and perverse? How much charity and compassion have we for our own weakness and sickness? How far can we build an inner society on the principle of love, allowing a place for everyone? And I use the term "cure of the shadow" to emphasize the importance of love. If we approach ourselves to cure ourselves, putting *"me"* in the center, it too often degenerates into the aim of curing the ego—getting stronger, better, growing in accord with the ego's goals, which are often mechanical copies of society's goals. But if we approach ourselves to cure those fixed intractable congenital weaknesses of stubbornness and blindness, of meanness and cruelty, of sham and pomp, we come up against the need for a new way of being altogether, in which the ego must serve and listen to and cooperate with a host of shadowy unpleasant figures and discover an ability to love even the least of these traits.

Loving oneself is no easy matter just because it means loving all of oneself, including the shadow where one is inferior and socially so unacceptable. The care one gives this humiliating part is also the cure. More: as the cure depends on care, so does caring sometimes mean nothing more than carrying. The first essential in redemption of the shadow is the ability to carry it along with you, as did the old Puritans, or the Jews in endless exile, daily aware of their sins, watching for the Devil, on guard lest they slip, a long existential trek with a pack of rocks on the back, with no one on whom to unload it and no sure goal at the end. Yet this carrying and caring cannot be programmatic, in order to develop, in order that the inferiority comply with the ego's goals, for this is hardly love.

Loving the shadow may begin with carrying it, but even

76

that is not enough. At one moment something else must break through, that laughing insight at the paradox of one's own folly which is also everyman's. Then may come the joyful acceptance of the rejected and inferior, a going with it and even a partial living of it. This love may even lead to an identification with and acting-out of the shadow, falling into its fascination. Therefore the moral dimension can never be abandoned. Thus is cure a paradox requiring two incommensurables: the moral recognition that these parts of me are burdensome and intolerable and must change, and the loving laughing acceptance which takes them just as they are, joyfully, forever. One both tries hard and lets go, both judges harshly and joins gladly. Western moralism and Eastern abandon: each holds only one side of the truth.

I believe this paradoxical attitude of consciousness toward the shadow finds an archetypal example in Jewish religious mysticism, where God has two sides: one of moral righteousness and justice and the other of mercy, forgiveness, love. The Chassidim held the paradox, and the tales of them show their deep moral piety coupled with astounding delight in life.

The description Freud gave of the dark world which he found did not do justice to the psyche. The description was too rational. He did not grasp enough the paradoxical symbolic language in which the psyche speaks. He did not see fully that each image and each experience has a prospective aspect as well as a reductive aspect, a positive as well as a negative side. He did not see clearly enough the paradox that rotten garbage is also fertilizer, that childishness is also childlikeness, that polymorphous perversity is also joy and physical liberty, that the ugliest man is at the same time the redeemer in disguise.

In other words, Freud's description and Jung's description of the shadow are not two distinct and conflicting positions.

Rather, Jung's position is to be superimposed upon Freud's, amplifying it, adding a dimension to it; and this dimension takes the same facts, the same discoveries, but shows them to be paradoxical symbols.

The same complementarity is true in regard to Freudian and Jungian rules of analysis. Freud had strict rules, and Freudians today continue with strict rules about the procedures of analysis, the relations between analyst and patient, and how the patient is to behave in the world during the time of his analysis. These rules are a new moral code, a new superego direction, modeled very much on the analyst's pattern of behavior and attitudes. Principally, they aim to guarantee that there will be a minimum of acting-out.

Because the forces of the shadow may be so dynamic on the one hand and so antisocial on the other, moral containment is required as long as the material which is being worked through has this primitive infantile shadow quality. However, from the Jungian point of view there is another reason for an analytical morality just as there is another aspect to the shadow. Morality reinforces the container within which the personality may transform. Let us look at this more closely.

Sexuality in particular is constellated by the shadow and takes on new life. Sexuality begins to carry the meanings of freedom and pleasure, of adulthood, potency, and creativity. The world becomes sexualized, and sexuality seems to confirm existence, to be ultimate truth in itself. Experiencing this aspect of the unconscious gives one the feeling that Freud was right through and through. Of course, the dangers of indiscriminate acting-out are immense. And a very difficult conflict breaks out between the new libido and the old morality. It seems as if this stage of working through the shadow has been occupying our society as a whole, especially in the last twenty years.

Other moral issues, such as aggression, anger, pride and

power, laziness, dishonesty and deceptive role-playing also belong to the shadows of feeling and also deserve consideration by a new morality. In analytical work these issues are no less urgent than sexuality. Yet because the new morality seems to make its case in terms of love and sexuality, and because love and sexuality are the contemporary banners under which even educational, legal, and political battles are fought, we are obliged to turn to this question too. Nevertheless, the real revolution going on in the individual soul is not so much sexual as it is psychic and symbolic, a struggle for a wholly new (yet most ancient and religious) experience of reality which only happens to be carried for us in its nascence by a sexual fantasy of this psychic reality.

Let us look first at the answer to the problems of love and sexuality given by the "new morality." The new morality appears to hold that fornication and adultery, as long as it is between consenting adults, as long as it is not in public, as long as it is meaningful and deep and not harming, as long as it is founded upon love, that is, recognition of the person of the other, is not morally wrong. In fact, Bishop Robinson says:

> . . . assertions about God are in the last analysis assertions about Love—about the ultimate ground and meaning of personal relationship.[3]
> Belief in God is the trust, the well-nigh incredible trust, that to give ourselves to the uttermost in love is not to be confounded but to be "accepted," that Love is the ground of our being, to which ultimately we "come home." [4]

Are "meaningfulness," "transcendence," "depth," and "harmlessness" adequate criteria for the justification of one's love, since upon this love fornication and adultery are justified? Or more—since upon these criteria God Himself is rec-

[3] *Honest to God,* p. 105.
[4] *Idem,* p. 49.

ognized? Are there not gradations of transcendence, so that all that lies on the other side of my ego's borders, all that transcends it, need not be called ultimate and divine? Is there love without involvement and involvement without harm? What do the myths of Cupid, of the Trojan wars, of history's great loving couples, of our own lives, tell us? Even if love gives meaning and healing, it opens new wounds as it closes old ones, and it provides no surety against its sometimes destructive wake.

Love can be taken at many levels, and the consulting room of the analyst or the pastoral counselor will be the ending place for many a love in which people have given themselves to the uttermost, met the ultimate, with noble intentions and deep feelings, asserting that their love was the ground of their existence, their sense of homecoming, even their experience of God and transcendence—and yet it all went wrong, dreadfully, horribly, sometimes suicidally wrong.

The question which we must raise against the "new morality" is not whether it is morally, or even theologically, sound or not, but rather whether it is *psychologically* valid. Is *Honest to God* true to life? By removing God from out there or up there to the depths, the most powerful and numinous image has been placed suddenly in the territory which was formerly the devil's dominion; and how are we to judge from whence come the impulses of love which call from these depths? How do we discriminate the spirits rising from the deep?

For let us make no mistake, the overwhelming emphasis upon personal relationships in the new morality—upon their depth, totality, and commitment—leads inevitably into the issue of sexual relationships. It is rare to have the one without the other, unless a great deal of psychological cultivation has been accomplished. By standing for the sexual implications of total commitment, at least the new morality is courageous. But again, is it psychologically valid?

Sexuality is not only a creative gift we bestow upon another, it is also a demonic force. Myths showing the cultivation of consciousness, such as the ones of Hercules and Ulysses, and the Gilgamesh epic too, as well as primitive initiation rituals, indicate that the demonic aspect is to be tamed or avoided, sacrificed or withstood. We must *know* something about the inner darkness which contaminates our love. The shadow aspect of sexuality—especially in our long-repressed culture—must first become freed of its incestuous components, must first become connected with love and relatedness, that is, must first be cultivated and developed. The new morality makes insufficient distinctions; it has one main criterion: *depth*. But the depth psychologist knows something about what lies down there. Dream images, fairy tales, and myths tell us enough of the netherworld of mother-imagos, of beasts and fires, of false brides and monsters, which must first be confronted by the hero before he is able to come into his kingdom and enter man's estate, before he is human and can understand what the Bishop of Woolwich means by love. Love romanticized is a sweet-cheat answer to the dried and technical world; love romanticized is only the reverse, the enantiodromia from boy-Faustian efficiency into left-behind school-boy longings. Only too often, as analysts and counselors know, in the noble aim of deep personal love when we would give our uttermost love we give our nethermost beast to someone else to keep for us.

To presume that every experience of love is Love of the Divine Ground of Being, to imagine that deep personal meaningfulness surmounts the pitch and hurdles of love's intricacies and can be the criterion for justification of unsanctified love, to be cozened into love by a philosophy which neglects its fearfulness (for if God is love, then the beginning of wisdom is the fear of love), and to call this naïve ignorance of the shadow side of loving "Honest to God" is witness just to how much of love lies in shadow. Better to call the new morality of loving "Naïve to God." A psychologist, lay in these matters of theology, nevertheless expects more from a "new reformation" than the mere replacement of a naïve God-image "up there" by a naïve love concept "in here." Although it is written that God is all love, does this mean that all love is God? When love is worshiped as God—and no matter the form this love takes, the lover who gives it, its heights or depths— have we not fashioned an idol, thereby crossing the second and third commandments? And are not these the commandments which bear more upon theological morality than the seventh and tenth, with which ministers today seem so fascinated? A psychologist must ask his clerical colleagues: why are you prey to these sophistries, these simple solutions; why do you blur the hierarchies of transcendence and ultimacy, neglecting the worlds of difference, represented traditionally by planes of being and classes of angels, between the levels and kinds of love; why do you traffic in hallucinogens, finding in them beatific visions; why do you confuse the voices of autonomous complexes with the Pentecostal gift of tongues; how can you equate falling-in-love with coming home to the God-head?

Love is more complex than its emotions, just as God is mystery, not enthusiasms. The differentiation of its complexities is a long initiation, only the beginning of which is falling into it, being ignited by its smoke and fire. Love would be elucidated: led into light. (In the same way, theology as the study of God is a long process of elucidation, a labyrinthine way.) We are ultimately helpless before the archetypal experience of love and we understand little; even its epiphanies are only openings into yet more possibilities of loving. No one would be bold enough to believe himself a theologian overnight, yet some claim as much for themselves after one night of love. And what of those who have not the power nor known that glory of giving themselves to the uttermost in love? Are they then cut off from the Kingdom? It

appears as if there is in the new morality of the new reformation an old doctrine of predestination, of "ins" and "outs":
in love or left out.

In other words, the new moraity for all its boldness in
giving to Jesus' message of love a vital modern interpretation
is not psychologically valid because it offers a general answer.
Yet there are no general answers effective in moral conflicts;
psychologically, moral conflicts are individually suffered
through crises which codes and preaching do not touch. In a
true moral conflict, which is the forge of personality and
character intensification, the individual is alone to hammer
out his own answer in his heart. The moral code is the anvil,
the individual crisis the hammer. For psychological culture,
what matters is that there be these conflicts. A morality which
would remove the source of conflict, ease the role of guilt,
and diminish the importance of being torn on the cross of
oppositions is no longer a morality but a new theological
tranquilizer called Love.

The analytical viewpoint supports moral codes because
moral codes perform two functions: first, they intensify conflict, without which consciousness is not possible; and second,
they favor internalization. The moral code is supported by
analysis not merely for the sake of outer morality, for social
form and ethics. Analysis is concerned with the development
of love, the eros, the sexuality within the individual. This
development is not favored by acting-out. As the shadow
side is not developed by repression, so is it equally not
favored by repression's opposite, acting-out. Repression and
acting-out are two sides of the same coin. A third way may
be called internalization, or symbolization, or living-in. Eros
is cultivated through intense internalization, perhaps the
most difficult of all activities, since eros by definition and
impulse leads us into the world and involvements with
others. Living-eros-in is therefore indeed an *opus contra*

naturam. The love impulse itself has within it the cultural seeds of internalization and symbolization; these are not sublimations imposed from above by will, reason, or social ethics. These cultural seeds are the self-governing, self-inhibiting regulation of instinct itself through conscience, ritual and fantasy. Love-poetry, love-letters, love-gifts, are all gestures not reducible to functional sexuality, but are, even among animals in the form of courtship and mating rituals, the dance and color of love itself. The liberating imaginative play which accompanies being-in-love is part of eros itself and points to the way in which the *opus contra naturam* is, paradoxically, also natural and instinctual.

All mystical discipline recognized the importance of internalization for the cultivation of eros and imposed intense strictures upon erotic life. I do not want to prescribe the practices of asceticism nor to proscribe living love as it happens in the world. Internalization is not the only way nor is it always the way, but a case and argument needs to be made for it since it has all but been forgotten in today's so-called sexual revolution and since it is in the main the analytical way. To point to the psychological significance of ascetic practices may therefore be useful, even if the practices themselves are not our concern. In studying them we are confronted with a universal awareness and archetypal teaching that the human being—as a distinction of his very humanity—needs to be initiated into love's mysteries. Yet if God is love, is this a wonder?

Traditional disciplines, of which alchemy was one, were mainly concerned with the transformation of consciousness, or what we might call personality development in the deepest sense. The redemption of the inferior personality, in particular the inferior eros—unlovingness, selfishness, attachment without involvement, vanity and superficiality, primitivity of sexuality and the sexualization of feeling, haste and compulsiveness, wasted energy in repetitive erotic fantasy—

84

is also a main concern of analysis. Therefore one can learn about personality development from these mystic disciplines such as alchemy.

In Chinese and Western alchemy, before one began the great *opus,* the experiment with one's nature, one had to search one's heart and examine one's moral attitudes. The cardinal virtues were recommended: health, humility, holiness, chastity, faith, hope, love, kindness, prayer, patience, moderation, and so on. In one way or another, these virtues came into alchemy again and again. It was an intensely moral business. Similarly intense moralities can be found in Yoga, in Catholic disciplines, in Sufism, in Shamanism, in Zen, etc.

There was a definite spiritual idealism, a strong moralism, and we must ask why this morality is necessary. The alchemist recognized the inner darkness, the shadow side of the personality, which was released when the eros aspect was undergoing transformation. Morality offered a containing bulwark against the corrosive, explosive, sulphuric sides of nature—that is, the repressed affects and desires. The moral principles were practical guides for dealing with the violent inner God. He, as *Solniger* or *Deus absconditus,* could demolish the creation from below just as the One on High sends down His locusts, lightning, and floods.

Morality as something imposed from above is derived from the theological model of a God-up-there. But this theological model is itself based on an archetypal idea, a statement of the psyche that something there is which is above and beyond itself. The soul is not all; there is something beyond it. If all statements are fundamentally reflections of the psyche, then the claims of the old theology that perfection is upward and that spirit is superior to psyche and body are admonitions of the soul to itself, saying, "Look up!" Placing God down in the deep will entail a new morality, perhaps. This morality will aim toward the transcendent immanent—that is, the deeply-within which is at the same time beyond. This within which is beyond is imaged in alchemy as the luminous eyes of the fish in the deep seas which are at the same time the distant stars above. The within which is beyond the Eastern language is the *suksma* aspect which is beyond the exoteric material level of things. In our language it is psychic reality beyond the ego level. The beyond within is the ultimate aim of the inner connection; a self-connectedness which is common to all beyond the ego. This realm of psychic reality always points beyond itself, transcends itself, and therefore it imposes a morality which demands a process of transcending, always going deeper, farther. We might call this the moral impulse of the individuation process. But wherever the ultimate value is placed, whether God is above or within, it is the "beyond" aspect which guides the moral impulse. Thus moral virtues remain as psychological imperatives, as calls from something beyond the ego, regardless of the locus of the theological God.

So in addition to the need for moral conflict, we now have the second psychological reason for morality. The development of personality itself imposes rules upon the ego. The personality as a whole demands that the ego as a part make sacrifices. The ego is limited by these values and principles, which are "super" ego in that they are above the ego, in that they transcend the ego. The process of transformation imposes these limitations upon the ego so that it can serve the process in the right way. In this light, these attitudes, these concepts of traditional morality, are transcendental values, as Kantian and Idealist philosophy has always held that the cardinal virtues are transcendental. However, from the analytical viewpoint they are psychologically transcendental. They are not hypostasized virtues floating around Heaven, or in a Platonic world, or in a Germanic metaphysical empyrean. They are rather the limitations and imperatives placed by the wholeness of the Self upon the ego to force it

86

to internalizations. As such they transcend the ego. They are experienced as transcendental by the ego so that transgression of them awakens guilt. This guilt is toward one's own possibility of self-realization, or self-redemption. The moral impulse of conscience therefore plays a significant role in the process of self-development.

Jung's essay on conscience was written toward the end of his life. It was published recently in English for the first time in Volume Ten of his *Collected Works*. He describes two forms of conscience. There is the conscience which we gain through learning, through the inculcation of values from our parents and our peers, from the traditional dogma of religions about right and wrong, and which we might call the superego. However, there is another sort of conscience, because, as he says, "The phenomenon of conscience in itself does not coincide with the moral code, but is anterior to it, transcends its contents. . . ." The superego, the first sort of conscience, is, in fact, secondary. I mean by this that we can only take in certain principles and follow a moral code and obey our parents' and our religions' teachings because of the psychological faculty of conscience, the inborn capacity to feel guilt. Conscience is a psychological function *sui generis*. Conscience is the voice of self-guidance. The self-regulating, self-steering activity of the psyche gives to conscience its authority. We may alter moral codes or even do away with morality, but we cannot do away with the psychological phenomenon of conscience.

Conscience, as an aspect of self-regulation, is the voice of the Self, which may and does conflict with the contents of a superego conscience. Then a man is led into the dilemma of individual conscience versus collective moral code, between conscience *per se* and its contents. This is the stuff of great literature and of daily counseling. Organized religion has long recognized this conflict of voices within, and has rightly called it a struggle between dark and light, evil and good. Unfortunately, organized religion has been too sure about which was the dark and which the light, too quick to identify its ethic with the good ethic.

I say "unfortunately" because in moral conflicts, good is often divided against itself; the Old King's voice of the super-ego and the voice of the Self yet-to-be-born who speaks through the Divine Child are both right. Out of these conflicts a new psychological standpoint can come, which we might also call a new morality. This psychological standpoint is a shift in position of the personality, away from one-sidedness and toward a more central truth. This truth admits, and then in time brings into conscious life, strands of the shadow which hitherto had not been allowed. Power drives become working ambition, deceits become social lies, fear of failure becomes open weakness, sexual fantasies become lived relationships. Integration of the shadow transforms the shadow. The qualities are no longer so dark when they are brought into the light of day and one has the courage both to give them rein and yet hold them in check. From the psychological point of view repression is not only an Evil and integration a Good, but repression is an origin of evil and integration a redemption of it.

The inner necessity which forces the Old King to alter his views speaks at first with the still small voice of individual conscience. In dreams, at times, it is a child in danger, ill, wounded, drowning, lost . . . or it can be an imprisoned criminal, a social outcast, an enemy alien, a man with another skin, creed, race, or an animal that cannot be destroyed, relentlessly pursuing like the Hound of Heaven . . . and one feels guilt, a sense of responsibility, a need to do something. Somewhere, there is a pressing necessity, and we are not doing what we should. This "should," for all its bearded, sick, childish, grotesque forms, is the growing side of ourselves: helpless without our care, young to challenge our nourishing heart, ill to constellate the nurse in us, pursuing because we run from it, in jail because we have judged it, dark because we have not let it into the light. This "should" is the command of the self-regulative function of the personality; each time we are being urged to realize a central core of the personality. Jung has called these dynamic centers the archetypes. The archetype particularly involved during the darkness is the archetypal shadow, none other than the Devil.

Confrontation with one's own darkness leads into those intense moral issues which are eternal, archetypal experiences of both growth and destruction. The human task in dealing with the shadow is to separate its strands by careful differentiation with thought and feeling of the experiences and images as they come, in order to release the disguised redeemer and to keep watch over the disguised destroyer. As the strands are usually so mixed, we cannot encourage the one without keeping one eye always on the Devil.

This brings us to a third and last psychological reason for morality: the struggle with evil. From the viewpoint of analytic practice, this third ground of morality is perhaps yet more important than the two already discussed: the need for moral conflicts and the need for internalizations.

The deepest level of the inner darkness, of the shadow, goes beyond your or my personal sins, crimes, negligences, and omissions. Below these are experiences of evil which cannot be humanized and which have been represented by devilish powers in the various religions of the world. We have lived through times in Europe in the thirties and forties —and they have continued in Algeria, in Tibet, in Southeast Asia and in the southeastern United States—which reveal the strength of these forces. Evil may well be a deprivation of the good theologically, but until the good comes on the scene, until the deprivation is restored, the experience of that evil is psychologically very real indeed. And the sufferer suffers not so much from a deprivation as from a very present, acutely effective evil. It is absolute, cruelly true there. Archetypal evil can neither be cured nor integrated nor humanized. It can only be held at bay. This point has been made with unremitting insistence by Dr. Adolf Guggenbühl-Craig in his Cutting Lectures at Andover-Newton Theological School. The experience of evil in forms of willful persecution, of vindictive victimizing, of destructive suffering, exploitation, physical pain and torment, have in them always something other than the demonic. "Something other" than the demonic can only be the human; it is the human element in the Devil that gives evil its full reality.

The demonic or diabolic in itself is arbitrary, mischievous, often a matter of luck or lot. It comes and goes and seems so senseless. The more that evil is archetypal, the more we experience it as impersonal. It is incomprehensible and we do not deserve it. (The same language has been used by recipients of God's goodness: "I am undeserving"; "it surpasseth my understanding.") Evil to some extent becomes more comprehensible and acceptable when it can be linked to something human, such as the sins of ancestral generations or the personal motivation of an enemy. When evil takes on godly form (Loki, Lucifer, Hermes-Mercury, the Trickster), it has a double nature and, like the spirit, it can blow for ill or good. It reaches its enormity only when it is half-human. When it is joined with the human ego, the will and reason and desire with which a man can choose a course of action and pursue an end, then does the merely devilish become truly evil. This implies that the archetypal shadow never achieves full actuality until it is linked in a pact with the human. And we are driven to conclude that the Devil too would incarnate in and through man.

Only morality defends me from this pact, from incarnating in my life, with my will and reason and desire, the Devil's intention. This leads one to appreciate anew the value of morality—for with what else but morality can the psyche protect itself against this force? In this sense, all morality does come from the Devil; morality is the psyche's answer to its own evil capabilities. Or, perhaps, at the level of inhuman power, we can hardly differentiate for sure between the sources of evil and morality. From the human standpoint, as met in the analytical session, the source of both seems to be the same: transcendent.

Arbitrary fateful happenings come from beyond as does the moral impulse itself. The events of fate can be humanized positively or negatively, as tragedies which ennoble us or as cruelties that sow destructive seeds into future generations. Human morality may not be able to alter the facts of fate, but it can at least prevent the archetypal shadow from direct incarnation. Human morality can and does protect from acting evil out, just as human kindness does soften fate's blows.

The Devil's power seems to grow not in our shadow but from our light. He gains when we lose touch with our own darkness, when we lose sight of our own destructiveness and self-deceptions. Theology says that pride leads directly to the devil; psychology can confirm this since, analytically seen, pride is a denial of the personal shadow and a blind fascination with the dazzle of one's own light. Therefore the best protection is not the reinforcement of the good and the light, but familiarity with one's own shadow, one's own devil-likeness. Homeopathic dosage of lesser evils as bitter pills of moral pain may be prophylactic against the greater evil. To err is human; to have shadow and be in shadow is human. To cast no shadow is possible only to the divine and the demonic. The human casts no shadow only at noon, only at the dazzle and zenith of his pride. But noon is also Pan's hour, so that at our greatest height we are in danger of the greatest fall. Pan drives out civilized morality in rebellious panic, intoxication and goatiness. He is not dead at all, but appears now as

Lucifer's heir, from below and within, as the ambivalent "prince of this world," bringing a confusion of vitality and darkness together, a monstrous mixture in the name of Dionysian renewal. Our obsessions with ecstasy, with rebirth through unconsciousness—whether through music, or LSD, or orgasm, or riots—show the paws and hoofs of Pan-Dionysos. Any psychology or theology which attempts the real depths will have to recognize Pan and his influence from these depths upon our love and upon our fear.

Finally, the reality of the shadow in counseling means that honesty is a grace that we cannot expect—neither from those who come to us and from ourselves to them, nor from anyone to God. The Devil and our devil-likeness means treachery, even when we have the best intentions. This is the reality of evil. Darkness is never dispersed as long as we are human and walk in the shadow of original sin and Lucifer is the original son. The lie and the cheat are ever present; and even honesty from God can be doubted, since in the case of Job He gave His ear to Satan. Facing the reality of evil, however, does not mean cynicism. It means merely that the optimism of honest-to-God be shaded in with the pessimism of psychological reality. To be honest-to-God we would first have to know a great deal more about truth—and what is truth? A hint toward knowledge of the whole truth might be found through a psychological reappraisal of the enigmatic robbers and thieves surrounding Jesus during his last human hours.

The reality of the shadow implies a recognition within the **individual counselor** of his own vast and collective unconscious, the shadows of his own soul, for just this ignorance of these shadows above all else has been responsible for the long decline of his profession and our faith. The tallest shade in these depths is the same today as always: that sin of pride, the identification with the Christ figure, which can come especially to the fore now in support of the role of pastoral counselor. Today the effects of this identification will be worse since it is a "dead God," one gone wrong, decayed, in the ferment of disintegration and resurrection, that catches the minister from behind so that he can no longer discriminate the spirits and tell who is behind whom: Christ, Devil or his own complexes. At the shadowy soft edges of the contemporary picture, Christianity and criminality may seep into each other. To the martyr-complex of the suffering-servant and the hero-complex of the soldier-of-Christ so much can be justified! When our time is in the dark confusion of Golgotha one need be only a degree or two off course, left or right, and one is kneeling before a thief.

The instrument which consciousness has in its hands for judging values, for holding to moral worth, for recognition of the human and personal in the best sense, for keeping connections going and flowing, for dignity and decency and kindness, is the function of feeling. If feeling gives the redeeming human touch, then the greatest danger is the capture and possession of feeling by the devil (in Mercuric capriciousness, in Satanic coldness, in wild affects of Pan). The moral sense has long been considered an attribute of the feeling function. Moral codes guard against deficiencies of feeling through emphasis upon manners and customs. Moral codes judge errors in the light of the intentions of the agent and the feeling context of situations rather than upon logical and empirical mistakes. So, too, psychopathy or sociopathic behavior, generally held as vicious or evil and once called moral insanity, shows itself in the deficiencies of feelings of guilt and feelings of loving participation in common humanity.

The dilemmas of the shadow[5] which I have touched upon in the last part of this chapter—that is, (1) separating individual self-regulatory conscience from revealed or collective superego conscience, and (2) separating the strands of the

[5] For more on the "dilemmas of the shadow" in mythology, theology, and psychology, see *Evil*, Northwestern Univ. Press, 1967.

shadow which can be lived and integrated from those which irredeemably belong in Hell—these two tasks lead into the wider realm of feeling. The education or cultivation of the feeling side in turn leads into our inner femininity, to which we shall now devote the last chapter.

IV

INNER FEMININITY:

ANIMA REALITY

AND RELIGION

WE HAVE been led to discuss the inner woman by many paths: befriending the dream and feeling rapport with the inner world, the passive attitudes of silence, stillness, acceptance and listening, the cultivation of eros and the perfection of love; and even the words for soul—*psyche* and *anima* —are themselves feminine in origin and connotation. So the subject of this chapter is the feminine, but the women that shall now occupy us are our own inner women, those female images and impulses passing through the corridors of the psyche, often neglected, sometimes cheapened, and certainly misunderstood. We cannot proceed further with a description of the experience of the unconscious or its connection to religion without becoming acquainted with this inner femininity.

In the dreams of men, a richness of women flows by. It is a defense against the feminine to try to reduce this grand spectrum to "Mother-substitutes" or "daughter-imagos." The usual view that the women in men's dreams reflect family figures needs to be expanded to include all the variety of the feminine which a man meets in the course of life.

Let us look at some of the more familiar images, beginning with that older woman who is school-teacherish, perfectionist, critical. For her, one can never do right, or enough, and in waking life one is continually under pressure to do better, to attack what has been done, or to fall into the complaining mood. She wants us to be better, yet in her urging for the best, she undermines the good that is. In the name of high ideals, she ends up convincing us of our worthlessness. We lose initiative and get lazier. How unfortunate it is when this inner woman becomes projected on someone nearby, for instance a wife, who then begins to act the role and even to look like the image nagging a man from his own unconscious.

This woman, so often presented as older than the dreamer, may have beneficent qualities too. There are figures—aunts, professional women, mature friends—who are encouraging, give one an ear, offer wisdom built on experience, with whom a relationship is possible without sexual involvement. They have a lofty position, one of authority and even of power, yet seem to rule by restraint and caution rather than by direct action. To label this image the "positive mother" is not enough. She continues to appear from time to time in a man's dreams, indicating his possibility for the development of his own wisdom, his own counsel, his own knowledge of life and how to handle it. There is a kindness in her, and a charity, and yet she accepts neither compromise nor delay.

A third figure, resembling the one just described, is too positive. She whispers simplicities of encouragement day and night, until a man believes he is really quite a remarkable figure, for she is in love with him—which means nothing

96

other than that he is in love with himself. We find her in dreams as someone rather worldly, often ambitious, often expensive and fast, but sometimes just the opposite: simple and dumb and good, but very much in love with the dreamer. She has the ability to turn him into a lion, a dominant, magnificent, and lazy roarer. There is pride and vanity, a striving for power, and empty conceit. This sort of encouraging positive female figure inflates only one side of the man—his externals, his persona, his worldliness. Although representing the anima, that is, the image of the soul, she actually leads a man away from its values and depths. She is the false bride who marries a man to the wrong values.

The values and depths of the soul are sometimes represented in dreams by a feminine figure without much character, with a nondescript face, a person from the past whom one hardly noticed and gave little credit to, and yet who reappears in various guises in dreams, waiting for attention, or worse, ill, in danger, dying. For it is up to me to do something for the neglected values and depths, etch out character through attentive interest, discern just what I have in me that remains undiscovered, give trust to values which have seemed until now to be of not much worth. Above all, the sick and lonely, poor and unwanted figure who is in danger is an image of the soul which presages depression, psychological poverty, perhaps even loss of soul. Her need constellates the heroic efforts of my ego.

This figure is usually presented by the unconscious as younger, which points to a part of us which is less mature. Positively seen, this means a potential which can grow and change, which carries something new, fresh, and hopeful; on the negative side, it is too-young, unawake, a pull backwards to adolescence. To go about with too wide a discrepancy between inner age and outer age is as much strain on the psyche as it is for a man to go about in public at forty with a high-school girl on his arm.

There is another favorite: the figure of the cool, pale blonde. She comes from remote regions such as Norway or Alaska, or has a wintry quality that is cold, distant, silent. She is aloof, and offers detachment and something spiritual and sublime. She can be very exciting in that her frigidity and distance activate a man to superhuman efforts of warmth and relatedness. This sort of anima can be felt by others as a coolness in emotional life, as if a man is somewhere aloof, hard to get at, uncaring even, despite appearances and despite what he says. He tends to fade away, to disappear into remote regions—all of which can be fascinating because it is so frustrating. He is difficult to attach and commit, as if he were not there in flesh and blood, as if his soul were something very rare and thin, like northern air or that fine-spun flaxen hair. Emotional life is withdrawn and secretive, and at the same time intensely passionate, for passion is not warmth; it is rather the blue flame constellated by ice.

Sometimes a whore appears in dreams and shows a man that he is in too-easy commerce with any passing spirit. His emotions do not react genuinely, but can be picked up for an hour or two and then forgotten. His feelings are for sale or at the call of others. Moreover, he does not value his own inner life of feeling beyond the kicks it gives him. His emotional promiscuity keeps him unmarried and uncommitted to his own self. In dreams this image is sometimes depressed, lonely, and abused. Because he misuses himself in this way, he is abused by others and abuses them. Relationships are based mainly upon the principle of usefulness. The old whore, on the other hand, can have a more positive meaning: she reflects a certain impersonality in human affairs, having been through it all and seen so much that nothing perverse astonishes. Her image tells a man of his own blend of cynical permissiveness, cheerfulness, and compassion.

The true materialistic vulgarities of a man's eros and soul values are represented less by the whore than by the collective popular images of entertainment and publicity. Like the Goddesses before, they too have their world-wide simultaneous epiphanies, but now projected in the darkened temples of a hundred thousand film theaters or flickering from the home altars of a hundred million television screens. With animal-headed consorts and castrated devotees they roam the continents. Everything not permitted mortals is allowed them. Their cult priests maintain their images with paint, relics, and manufactured legends. Their vast commercial success replaces a man's inner personal failure. The more the inner woman is represented by images of the film or fashion industry, the more collectively common, the more just like everyone else's will be that man's soul qualities. The prettier the anima, the less beautiful may be the soul; the more popular the image, the less individual a man's form of relating; the more sexually attractive the collective Goddess, the less chance a man has to free himself from Ishtar's animal complusion, to disengage soul and flesh.

The girl who is a bird is another familiar figure of the mythology of the inner feminine. Perhaps she is pink and fancy in a ball-gown or downy baby underwear, but whatever the fluffy encasement she is an ethereal creature flitting through the air. She takes a man on magic flights of fantasy, puts him in the rosy glow of optimism, and fills his head with the feathery thoughts of pseudo-philosophy and impractical schemes that have no substance and are blown about by every current of opinion. A man has trouble settling down and brooding; he always hears the sirens singing somewhere else. This sentimentally romantic image can be placed upon an outer woman so that she begins to live as baby-doll, bird-brained and fantastic.

Her opposite has feet of clay, is mud itself. The reduction of the anima to mere matter, to a woman from the backwoods, is also an image of our dreams. That thick-thighed, big-breasted peasant, dumb and slow and half-cretin, reflects the low position relegated to the feminine by the intellectual of the city. She belongs only in the kitchen, or back of the barn where he can tell his obscene jokes and make unfeeling insulting remarks with her full uncouth approval. Woman or animal, front or back, mother or wife—it is of no consequence. This image of an archaic earth soul is the ugly, materialistic, and uncreative counterpart to that modern man locked in his high and dry structures of cynical, critical, and technical sophistication.

A more positive counterpart of modern ego-consciousness is the girl of an older culture. She may be Jewish, Egyptian, Mediterranean, Chinese, and she points to a layer in time before sensuousness and spirit are split apart. She too connects to the earth, to some solid background of tradition out of which new things can grow. Her image is accompanied by the experience of historical depth. She is a repository of human warmth and gives the sense of ancient meanings, the sense that one has a long inner past, a soul entangled in antiquity, which if allowed across the threshold has in it a cultured wisdom able to intuit underlying patterns far more imaginatively than can the up-to-date ego.

Another of the more usual figures is the young and seductive girl, sometimes tawny-skinned, sometimes nude, often dancing or swimming—that is, associated with color, body, music, and water. Her hair is a marked feature and may be the only part we distinctly recall on waking. She may be aggressively pursuing or she may be quietly fascinating, but she mobilizes libido and her appearance is a call. She knows the secret of play, and has pagan or heathen associations of another religion and moral system. Sometimes she is on an island, closed in or simply "unable to come out"; sometimes she is unreachable by telephone, the line is cut; sometimes she is associated with animals or is half-animal. Often she has an interesting father—as the legends where there is only a princess and a powerful king—repeated in our dreams today by the college girl who reappears, perhaps herself not so interesting, but who, when one remembers, did have a father of significance.

This image alone tells us a great deal; it is what Jung calls a typical anima figure. It is associated with animal and water life—that is, with the instincts, with the flow of emotion, liquidity, and rhythm, with nature and physical pleasure. Her fascination and compelling attraction point to the importance of this element for one's psychic completeness. (For we may remember that as when I am chased in a dream, it means as well that I am running away, so when something is attractive it means as well that this aspect of the psyche wants attention. When I do not pay attention to the unconscious, then the inner world uses seduction to make the ego pay attention. The seductive motions of the enchantress catch my sexual energy.)

The significant father who stands behind the anima-figure reveals in part why her influence is so compelling. Behind her, or rather through her, one is led into one's own full fatherhood, one's own masculinity. In other words, the way to the larger, stronger, firmer manhood is through intimate association with one's inner femininity. One cannot sidestep this confrontation, avoid the anima, since it will only become more unruly, more seductive, and more demanding.

Since men do live psychologically in a harem, it is useful to get to know one's inner household. We do well to know by what fascination we are bewitched: turned into phallic animal, petrified into immobility, or lured underwater and away from real life. We do well to know whom we are unconsciously following in counsel, where our Cinderella sits in dirt and ashes or Snow White lies in poisoned sleep, what hysterical feminine tricks we play deceivingly on ourselves with affects and moods, which Muse inspires or Beatrice ignites and which is the true favorite who moves the deepest possibilities of our nature and holds our fate.

101

All these women are images of the anima, of the soul. Through them is revealed a man's internal life, his personal relationship to himself and to what is beyond himself. In as much as they express my responsiveness and inwardness, they also present forms in which my religious life unfolds. If my soul image is too young, or too cold, or too materialistic, or too critical, then there will be corresponding distortions of my religious life. The soul in tradition was Christian (*anima naturaliter christiana*) but the anima in modern man may be anything but. Without this confrontation with the inner feminine, the confessional affiliation of even the clergyman may affirm only his commitment on the ego level. Within and below much else may be going on.

There is another way of approaching one's inner femininity, and that is through the emotion or the mood. As we have already noted, we stumble upon the unconscious through dreams and fantasies, but also in affects.

Some affects are particularly feminine in nature—for example, self-pity, sensitivity, sentimentality, the sense of weakness and despondency, depression. It is not that these affects particularly pertain to women. (On the contrary, the affects of women are usually more masculine: causes, opinions, principles, arguments of all sorts expressed through her lawyer/salesman/policeman/preacher/statesman animus. Sometimes it just smashes things, slamming doors and giving other exhibitions of the bullfighter/discus-thrower/six-day bike-rider/trapeze-artist.) Self-pity, depression, sentimentality, and the sense of despondency are feminine in that to a man they feel feminine. They do not have "go-ahead" in them. They lessen a man's ability to achieve, just as arguing and fighting often lessen a woman's ability to connect. Therefore the familiarity with one's own femininity may have to take the course of a journey through some of the

102

places visited by the Pilgrim in John Bunyan's *Pilgrim's Progress.*

Only within intimate situations will men reveal this inner femininity, this sensitive, delicate, touchy spot. Particularly difficult is *self-pity.* When people come to us, they are often despondent and perhaps too maudlin and ready with self-pity: the unjustly accused in a married dispute, the hard-working father who has to have the wrong sort of son, etc. But there is a self-pity which is perhaps harder to realize because it is harder to admit. This differs from the self-pity which is rather a self-justification and defense. It is harder to realize, I think, because of the long tradition supported by the churches.

The clergy have long urged that I must love my neighbor, but this love has too often been at the cost of loving myself —especially since this self of mine is blemished from the beginning with sinfulness. Love has been put on me as a demand, an exhortation to love neighbors and even enemies, to love where I cannot and do not feel love. Even where my love does not flow, I am nonetheless urged to will love into action. But the development of the feeling side of the personality often begins not where it is supposed to begin, not with feeling for another person. Rather, it often begins in shadow, with self-pity, with feeling for oneself. From the need for caressing and tenderness, to be taken up and listened to and cared for, there comes the real caring for oneself. Self-pity is the beginning of caring deeply about oneself. And through self-pity I can be led to rediscover a host of neglected values in myself which have waited for this plunge into yearnings for redemption, into lost aspirations and regrets over wrong choices. For self-pity is a form of self-discovery, self-revelation; it reveals my longings to myself. What really matters to my deepest, most vulnerable and touchy part is revealed. It is a beginning of extending downward the vertical connection.

The sentimentality and bathos which assails us takes us back again to earlier days, college songs and their words, the girl we never made, the rejections and hurts and betrayals. Unless reopened and felt afresh, these repressed remainders become the very barriers which separate adults from their own teen-age children. The incestuous impulse is intensified by one's unredeemed adolescent longings to join again a world which is split off and carried in the unconscious by the images of the too-young girl. Moving toward one's teen-age children is less problematic when one is no longer threatened by the teen-age child within.

Perhaps sadness is a better word than despondency. It is more familiar and simple. Despondency has its antidote: more heart, more spirit, more faith, more effort. But sadness is an increasing undertone, the lengthening shadow on the sundial as the day moves toward evening. This sadness seems to be a complaint of men, a statement of their feminine side as they grow older. It is as if women carried sadness with them consciously as part of their feminine sense of reality, since they are usually more aware of the reality of aging anyway. But then a man reaches thirty-five or forty, or sometimes not until near fifty, and he feels sad; there is a weight on the heart and no matter what he does it does not go away. This is typical of an anima state, an anima mood, the steady accompaniment of the soul which has become a burden since it has not been given what it needs. This is the time when he is most vulnerable for the love affair which may or may not solve something; and should it solve the enduring undertone of sadness it will prove only a short-term alleviation unless the relationship does something for the feminine side of himself, cultivating it, letting it express itself, and even more, reorienting his usual habitual masculine point of view in terms of the feminine values of life. For just this—the reorientation of the masculine point of view—seems to be the purpose of these feminine emotions which depress and weaken us.

They peel off our crust, they soften our heart, they sap our right arm in favor of the left where we are awkward and unable to manage. If all psychological events have intentionality, they move toward some meaning. The disturbance to masculine consciousness of the feminine would then have for its meaning the weakening and feminization of the usual point of view. This implies that after mid-life, providing that life up to its midpoint has seen a certain masculine development, the way is not the continuation along the same line, "more of the same," but rather the extension of the personality through its opposite. One aspect of the ego's opposite we saw in the previous chapter: the dark side of the shadow; the other aspect faces us now: the inner femininity.

Let us connect these psychological observations on personality development with the feminine symbols and patterns in religious experience. Let us amplify further aspects of the feminine side as exemplified in comparative religion.

The Shaman, of whom Eliade has written an extraordinary book,[1] in some cultures performs in the course of his initiation into the mysteries of his priesthood a ritual and symbolic change of sex, including transvestism and homosexuality, living as a wife to another man. He is called a "soft man" or a "man similar to women." The integration of one's female side through living it out in a ritual can be found in Siberia, Patagonia, and Indonesia, and among Asiatic Eskimos and American Indian tribes.

The greatest of the Greek exemplary figures, Hercules, that man of men, that hero of heroes, after completing his twelve labors served Queen Omphale. After the process of becoming a conscious man through the laborious effort of struggling through task after task was over, Hercules did not go on to greater heights and glories. He went mad; and more important for our theme, he was a servant to a woman. There

[1] M. Eliade, *Shamanism* (London and New York, 1964).

are vase images of him in women's clothing. Later variations of the mythologem have Hercules doing women's work, spinning at the Queen's bidding.[2]

Ulysses, on his ten-year journey back from the wars, again a hero of more than human size, the faithful husband and wily leader of men, passed a whole year on Circe's isle, abandoning his urgent journey, the goal of his captaincy, to the joys of her table and her bed; then ornamented, girded, attired by that female hand, he delayed and reoriented his course, gaining thereby foreknowledge, help, strength, and wisdom to meet the next phases of his journey homeward.

An amplification in reverse would be that of Orpheus. Orpheus is perhaps the earliest statement in Western culture of a non-worldly religion, where the rewards are in another life, another world. After the death of his wife, he shunned all women, refusing to initiate them into the mysteries or to allow his followers to take part in the Dionysian celebrations, which had a marked feminine component. Orpheus' reward for being a misogynist was death at the hands of women. They brutally beat him to death and tore him apart. The feminine side—nature and the dance of life imaged in the Maenads—which he denied, returned, as the repressed always returns, and killed him with raving passions. Against these feminine forces not even his music or his otherworldly ascetic religion was defense.[3]

In the statuary of Hinduism, the female aspect, as the vitality or Shakti, is represented as a distinct image with its own attributes. He who worships Shiva (or Krishna and Vishnu) worships as well the various Goddesses associated with the incarnations of the God. Contemplation and worship of the feminine brings with it exhilaration and love of life, for its rhythmical changing beauty is an essential even if paradoxical part of ascetic Shaivism.

[2] K. Kerenyi, *The Heroes of the Greeks* (London, 1959).
[3] *Idem.*

The Buddha's feminine characteristics are obvious: the heavy, silent, full-bellied, soft-breasted receptivity; the huge ears, open and taking in; the tree under which he sits and the lotus posture; compassion.

The amplifications of integrated femininity in the Judeo-Christian religion are well known. Let us nevertheless review—only as hints and indications—a few themes. The Sabbath in Jewish tradition is feminine. It is welcomed on Friday evening as a female guest, as a Queen, bringing joy. It is a time for comfort and ease at the end of work, time for the senses, for relationship—the feminine side—and hence has become the time for family. In the Kabbala one side of the tree of the ten Sephirot, the side of God's mercy or love, is feminine, as is too the Sechinah, the mystical body of Israel, the People as a unity, the People as God's chosen bride, or vagrant harlot, the land of Zion, and all longed-for, not-yet-attained images of fulfillment. For it is as a woman, the psyche in its female form, that the soul receives and knows God.

The importance of women in the New Testament is too familiar to dwell upon, as is the swelling importance of women and feminine symbolism in the passion of Jesus. Of all Jesus' strengths, above all the strength of his *weakness,* stands out his sympathy and understanding for human weakness. "Jesus wept." There is also no need to enter into Mariology, or the litany or the symbolism of roses, gardens, wells, palms, lilies, associated with the archetypal image of Mary. But it is worth recalling that the Holy Ghost, now usually conceived as another masculine aspect of the Trinity, has for its image—even of the Holy Spirit—the dove, which once belonged to Aphrodite and which meant, throughout the ancient world, Love and the Goddess who is that love's inspirer.

During the Renaissance, many aspects of the story of Jesus were taken up in painting. One particular image seemed to draw the interest of painter after painter, century after century: the Annunciation. There Mary is depicted as a young childish innocent, carefully dressed and set down in a walled interior—nothing more than a schoolgirl at home in her room, often doing handwork or at her studies, who is suddenly confronted with the Angel. In her body redemption will be prepared. She is shocked, astonished. In her face horror and rejection mingle with acceptance.

This motif occurs in men and women today. In that schoolgirl image of our dreams, in those too-young emotions—too naïve, too innocent, too self-centered—something redemptive can grow, which might in the end lead to our own redemption, and to the maturing of the feminine side toward that figure of wisdom and compassion which Mary becomes at the end of the story. But in the beginning it is astonishment and shock, for somewhere we are all virgins, sensitive, shy, psychologically naïve, unexplored in our emotional life, unwilling to be called into involvements, unawakened to the terribleness of truth, resistant to the major challenge, preferring where it is safe, at home, familiar and protected, with books or bits of handiwork, kindly, charitable, obedient, well-meaning. Yet from all this goodness little can come unless the psyche's womb receive the fiery seed of one's own unique essence which fulfills its creative longing and from which inner fertilization issues the experience of renewal.

This condensed description has aimed to give an indication *why* the cultivation of one's own world of image and mood, of feeling and fantasy, of one's own garden, is essential for what might be called the religious moment. Because the religious moment requires a passive mood to God's intentions, a receptive state to Divine Will, a wounding experience which opens us, it is feminine in nature. Although I may have said something about the what and the why, the question which remains is *how*.

108

How does one come to terms with this feminine side; how does one cultivate it? How does one develop the inner barrenness that can conceive no new start, the schoolgirl virginity that plays at life, the cold spinster or impatient harlot? The simplest answer, the way which is most general and happens most often is: with and through women, intimacy and intercourse with women. Unfortunately, this statement is taken naïvely, upon its literal face. If the human connection between people depends to some extent on the inner connection within people, then the same will be true for the development of the feminine side. Honesty may mean directness, but surely "honest to God" does not mean direct to God. That is naïve, and just as naïve is the belief in the direct approach of the promiscuous solution to differentiate the femininity of the psyche.

Sexual intimacy and intercourse become compelling very often when all other forms of intimacy and intercourse have broken down; similarly, when interest in the feminine side of oneself is neglected, when one shows no concern to learn from or to change one's anima states of mood and temper, of taste and manner, then does the outer woman become the only way to learn. Love cannot be accurately defined, so the reasons why two people meet and fall in love—in spite of all the world literature dedicated to this theme and the psychological case studies documenting its details—have yet to be catalogued. But one thing is certain: when two people are moved toward each other, there is a fall or call or pull into union with an unknown, whether heavenly or hellish, which through this union becomes familiar and intimate. But there are other ways than the sexual to find familiarity and intimacy with the unknown.

My point is not to argue for or against individually determined sexual relationships. This debate to a psychologist has little substance, since people live their lives according to their own most obscure and individual patterns of reasoning.

(Besides, the system for regulating the relations between the sexes, because it is the fundamental expression for regulating the relations of the opposites, is subject to infinite variety, from strict and life-long abstinence and seclusion to legalized incest, polygamy and child-spouses, any of which models provide justification for almost any sort of behavior.)

Often, too, the green pastures of an affair are a way of avoiding the constricting sterility of a marriage. If we should try to find where love is most torn and tormented today it would seem to be in modern Western marriages, as if to say that the crucifixion of love, of Christ, is to be found right in our own homes, in the intolerable situation of marriage to which many are nailed. Modern marriage carries an immense burden without vessel of living sacrament or support of tradition. If this is a Gethsemane, then to go to sleep pretending it is a quiet garden or to walk out on the impossible agony of marriage, actually experienced as the very death of love by so many who come for counseling, would be to walk out, separate, or divorce from the place where Christ as love actually is. Held through the night, it may indeed only lead to more pain. On the other hand, can love not resurrect?

We have the opportunity to live the union of opposites and cultivate eros every day in marriage. A good marriage would mean a good union. But such a union is mainly reserved for those couples where each fits exactly into the other's missing parts. The "good" marriage is therefore at the expense of individual wholeness. The sort of union represented by the "good" marriage prevents development, for my mate blocks me from filling in my own lacunae with my own growth. She is already there ahead of me, habitually, competently. In marriage, two halves do not make a whole; so that there can hardly be "good" marriages until there are first "bad" marriages, that is, where the individual's process toward wholeness produces needs often contrary to the usual image of a "good" marriage.

110

Marriage as the sanctification of the mystery of the couple has no handbook. Some of its problems, but never its mystery, may nevertheless be referred to that model of the cross of love described in Chapter I. Often one or the other axis is overloaded, and marriage crises refer to the re-adjustments in proportions between love as active communication and love as inward depth. Sometimes it happens that love as a state of being grows in the barren acres left where love as desire burnt itself out. Sometimes this is impossible. It is safe to say only that marriage can be a miracle in the midst of the daily if attention is given perhaps less to each other and "our marriage problem" and more to the feminine qualities within ourselves, man or woman. It is said that marriage is three-quarters the responsibility of the woman, which means that the feminine carries the larger part of marriage. But the feminine is in both, man and woman. It is the man's loss of anima and his overcompensated mother-boundness, and the woman's aging away from her femininity, that quick-dry-freeze the couple into instant husbands and wives so archetypally similar everywhere, harsh, bitter, without specific taste, yearning for the water of life which each hopes to find through a new experience.

But there are other ways of gaining knowledge of the feminine and of discovering one's other side. Because this psychological truth is often lost today, it deserves emphasis. The distaff side is not only outside; it is also within, for only a slight preponderance of chromosomes makes us male. That chaste and shy man, D. H. Lawrence, discovered women to themselves intimately and validly without having first to pillage the countryside for personal research. The development of sensitivity and feeling is only in one aspect sexual, and then sometimes in the last, rather than at the first. Mainly it seems a matter of timing.

Curiously, when sexuality is lived in for a while as fantasy instead of acted out, erotic life is given the opportunity to undergo re-mythologization or re-sacralization. It tends to take on a new consecration through its containment by the psyche. When the heat is held the psyche can be ignited into imagination. And, at the same time, the psyche, as anima or soul, gives the human touch. It provides the feminine form and feeling differentiation, expanding urges into love. Sometimes this quickening, this re-sacralization of sexuality is ushered in with cosmic *welt-schmerz,* with body-sensations in the chest, with dream women in blue and their eyes, with fascination with Woman as such—all of which have given rise to and been differentiated through the cult of the Love Goddess as well as by theories of cosmogonic eros, the harmony of the spheres, and the spiritualization or divinization of love. The archetypal origin of all seems to be the self-inhibition of eros, which is neither a prohibition nor a moralistic restraint. Sexuality is neither condemned nor acted out, nor is it sublimated into something else. Sexual feelings and fantasies are lived vividly within the person; then, through a feminine image they can spread, like light or like odor (hence the classical religious symbols of the "celestial flower of divine love") out into the universe. The lover loves all the world as the world loves him.

But once reconsecrated by these higher realms, love homes downward again to the middle region which is simply the human psyche, calling for something human for its fulfillment. Falling out of love is falling into humanity. The higher reaches of eros, just as its lower, are utterly unconcerned with human love and the human person. In itself, sexuality is impersonal. Sexual eros is a brutal demon or a winged god compelling us out of the human unless it be united with and contained by the psyche. Bringing cosmic exhilaration down to earth again, letting it become human and incarnated and thereby reconsecrating the mundane, may or may not require an actual other person, but always this process of psychization takes time.

Another way for the cultivation of eros within oneself requires that one be open to the unconscious as already discussed. Am I willing to go where I stumble upon it, especially where I am attracted—not only to that person but especially to that person's image? This is the radical internalization of eros: one treats the outer as if it were inner, "only a dream." One lets oneself be dreamt along, yet retaining a consciousness within these movements. Also, one follows one's dreams, those spontaneous natural bridges thrown up every night between consciousness and the other side. The more remote we are and the darker the abyss between day and night, the more tempting and seductive will be the images to lure us. The psyche uses the seductress when the ego is unwilling to move. The proud warrior hard of heart and hard of hearing is called by sexual fantasies. These are often the only way the unconscious can make itself felt and heard.

Openness to the dream implies openness to every dream and dream fragment, every image. It is a convenience of the ego to decide in the morning which dreams are of use and which dreams are not, which can be happily forgotten and which are important. Too often the ego's decision of what is important serves only the ego and the ego's importance, whereas a major function of the dream is making the ego relative within the psyche as a whole. This often feels to the ego like a negative humiliation, even though it can also be a positive humbling. If the ego is allowed to choose among the dreams, a subtle form of self-treachery begins, leading to one-sidedness and eventual inflation or depression. The energy is not balanced. To take the unconscious seriously means to listen to as much of it as one can and not only to the parts which are pleasing.

Despite all earnestness, the assimilation of dreams depends—as we have already discussed in regard to the shadow—upon playful acceptance of their incomprehensibility. Again, we have a paradox: arduous analysis of them coupled with foolish submission to them. Though I must work at recapturing my dreams, without the playful feminine indirectness and patient feminine indecisiveness little will be assimilated. The integration of dream and consciousness takes something besides effort.

The technical method by which the inner world of dream and image is cultivated—the internalization of eros, to call it by another name—is briefly described in three phases. At first, it is an attitude of consciousness to accept what comes, yet not to act this out. From the energetic viewpoint alone it is easy to see how this will increase the realm of psychic reality, for much is flowing in and nothing is flowing out. Of course the fantasies that flow in—as desires, projects, impulses—are all urges to action. It is indeed a difficult task to separate the fantasy from its dynamic root, its urge to action. We tend either to repress everything because it cannot be brought into life, or, if we do allow fantasy in, then we want to live it out immediately.

This method inhibits the ego as "doer." Nevertheless, consciousness can be extended although the ego be thwarted. Consciousness may even grow at the expense of the ego, if we keep to a difference between consciousness as reflection and consciousness as action.

Here we may remember how the ego grows. The ego develops its focus from infancy onward by gathering to itself the more diffuse light of general consciousness. Its growth is at the expense of the whole being, of the Self. On the one hand, this development gives the ego its force for specialized directed attention and action. But on the other hand, this development robs consciousness from the psyche as a whole, leaving much of it in the dark. (Archetypal ego-figures showing how the ego-complex often gains its consciousness are frequently thieves: Eve, Jacob, Hermes, Prometheus.) The continued intensification of consciousness to the ego and by the ego causes more and more darkness, more and more uncon-

114

sciousness elsewhere. The diffuse consciousness of the land-in-between narrows to the specifications of the ego or falls into the abyss. We lose our ability to see in the penumbral world, and lost too is the child's sense of wonder. Therefore the symbolic function falls away as the ego develops and the world becomes demythologized. Demythologized religion simply reflects our modern consciousness that has been narrowed to the ego only. To become as a child and to be led by a child means to reverse the process of ego development, to abandon the ego focus of consciousness.

The difference between consciousness as reflection and consciousness as action is also not just the difference between introversion and extraversion. The action of the ego may be introverted as well as extraverted, for we may indeed be introvertedly ego-active, harrying, worrying, searching our inner life along with curiosity. So, too, extraverted life may be reflective, as the fool wanders through the world. The extension of consciousness to which I refer here is more the deepening of the vertical direction, the inner connection with oneself. The light is playful and wavering. Its starting point may be the world or oneself, but it moves toward no decisions, toward no narrowing of ego-focus. As this inner world of fantasy increases through sacrifice of the animal compulsion of the ego to act, a kind of contained inner space develops, that realm mentioned at the end of Chapter II. In short, the first phase is the inhibition of ego activity for the sake of fantasy consciousness. One feels regressed, weak, dependent, indecisive and childish.

After having accepted fantasies with their impulses and their regressions and having at the same time refrained from acting them out in the world, the second phase is to give energy back to the fantasies, to activate them, to endow them with enough libido, interest, attention, and love, so that they take on a vivid spontaneous life of their own.

The cultivation of fantasy, even should it be impelled by

covetousness and lust, rather than a contradiction of Exodus 20:17 and Matthew 5:28 is perhaps their exegetical amplification. I can indeed look upon an object with desire and cultivate that desire, watching it, feeling it, letting its imaginary possibilities run away with my mind, entertaining its delight, without acting it out. A separation may be made between inner and outer, between desire contained in the subject and desire acted out upon the object, between the left-hand of feeling-filled images and needs and the right-hand of desirous demands. Thus it is the right eye and the right hand which offend and are to be sacrificed (Matthew 5:29), for the right side is the side of action. Fantasy leads straight into action only when there is not enough space between idea and impulse, when the inner realm is so cramped that nothing can be contained for long. What I see, I want; what I want, I must get. Every need becomes a demand. If fantasy is to be restrained by reference to its relation to the outer world, to criteria of "reality-testing" about what can be realized in direct action, then it loses the name and nature of fantasy altogether. Fantasy has nothing to do directly with the concrete world. It is neither reducible to it in origin nor aimed toward it in purpose. Fantasy may take its instigations from outer events and then manipulate those events in mind, but its realm is purely imaginary. So, too, the lust and covetousness are imaginary—that is, they are psychic dynamisms, impulses of the soul, which would be ludicrously short-circuited were they directly to enter the world. These impulses appear not so much in order to be sated as appetites by action, but to create the inner realm, to enlighten the soul's insights, to give it play and dimension, to set it free from concrete limitations upon the possible, and thus to deepen and enrich its scope of experience.

As was said above in Chapter III, the real revolution in the soul is not in itself sexual. The human sexual instinct is widely plastic and provides energy for changes in consciousness all through psychological history. If one may read the trend of collective events through the particular experiences of individuals, the deep change now going on is merely carried by sexual fantasies as psychic dynamisms, the intention of which is ultimately a revivification and expansion of psychic reality. Through living-in rather than only acting-out immense instinctual energy is given to inner life. The lust and covetousness give the impetus to discover inner space, just as there must be such strong psychic dynamisms as curiosity and competitiveness and science fiction fantasies to drive us to the moon, Mars, and Venus of outer space.

That a person reacts with fear and shame to his own fantasies shows that still not enough separation is made between subjective experience of oneself and objective action. The fear and shame are protective; these emotions keep one from acting out, from venting these fantastic passions upon the world. The fear and shame also give conviction and reality to the inner world. It is not only a "mere fantasy" or "daydream."

The interest in fantasy is a mark of most spiritual disciplines, whether as psychological method in Jung's "active imagination," or in the techniques described in alchemical mysticism or in Christian, Hindu, Persian, and other texts. But never is passive fantasy enough; for fantasy is endless, spinning a veil, confusing image and action. The phase beyond fantasy is imagination, which is the work of turning daydreams and fantasies into scenic inscapes wherein one can enter and which are peopled with vivid figures with whom one can converse and feel, and touch their presence. This, then, would be psychological insearch. Such imagination costs great effort. The work of converting fantasy into imagination is the basis of the arts. It is also the basis for the new steps we take in life, since the visions of our personal futures come first as fantasies. Again, there is reason for holding them in at the beginning, imagining them into rich detail and large-scale schemes, before deciding whether they are to be attempted in the world or further followed internally, lived out or lived in.

Imagination and its development is perhaps a religious problem, because imagination becomes real only through belief. As theology tells us, belief is an act of faith, or it is faith itself as a primary investment of energy in something which makes that something "real." Inner life is pale and ephemeral (just as is the outer world in depressed states) when the ego does not turn to it, believe in it, and endow it with reality. This investment, this commitment to inner life, increases its importance and gives it substance. The interest one pays soon pays interest. The frightening forces become gentler and more manageable, the inner woman more human and reliable. She no longer only seduces and demands; she begins to reveal the world into which she draws one and even gives an account of herself, her function and purpose. As this "she" becomes more human, the moods one is subject to become less difficult and personal and are replaced by a steadier emotional undertone, a feeling-tone, a chord. No longer in conflict with her, more energy is now disposable to consciousness, which shows that the energy spent in this discipline comes back in a new form. However, as in a physical system, no more can come out than is put in. Only devotedly faithful attention can turn fantasy into imagination.

This faithful attention to the imaginal world, this love which transforms mere images into presences, gives them living being, or rather reveals the living being which they do naturally contain, is nothing other than the "re-mythologizing" of which we spoke at the end of Chapter II. Psychic contents become "powers," "spirits," "gods." One senses their presence as did all earlier peoples who still had soul. These presences and powers are our modern counterparts of former pantheons of living beings, of animated soul parts, protective household gods, and ominous demons. These beings were "mythical" in that they were part of a "tale" or psychic drama. The same archetypal dramas are played in us and by us, and through us for our behalf, once the imaginal aspect of our lives and of life itself is given attention. Attention is the cardinal psychological virtue. On it depends perhaps the other cardinal virtues, for there can hardly be faith nor hope nor love for anything unless it first receives attention.

There is a further consequent of the credit one pays to the images of the soul. A new feeling of self-forgiveness and self-acceptance begins to spread and circulate. It is as if the heart and the left side were extending their dominion. Shadow aspects of the personality continue to play their burdensome roles but now within a larger "tale," the myth of oneself, just what one is which begins to feel as if that is how one is meant to be. My myth becomes my truth; my life symbolic and allegorical. Self-forgiveness, self-acceptance, self-love; more, one finds oneself sinful but not guilty, grateful for the sins one has and not another's, loving one's lot even to the point of desire to have and to be always in this vivid inner connection with one's own individual portion. Such strong experiences of religious emotion seem to be the gift again of the anima. This time she has a special quality that might best be called Christian and which only begins to reveal itself—this *anima naturaliter christiana*—after long attentive care has been given to much of the psyche that might not be Christian.

The third step is gratuitous. It refers to the free and creative appearance of imagination, as if the inner world now come to life begins to act spontaneously, by itself, undirected and even unattended by ego-consciousness. The inner world not only begins more and more to take care of itself, producing crises and resolving them within its own transformations, but it also takes care of you, your ego-worries and ego-claims. This is the feminine Shakti of India at a higher state;

it is also the nine Muses responsible for culture and creativity. One feels lived by imagination.

Another clue as to how inner femininity can be cultivated is given by the mythologems. Hercules serves the feminine principle. This implies that one lets oneself be ruled at times by the moon, the night, reflection, reaction, the owl and the pussycat—rather than by the sun and its straight, direct, honestly clear consciousness and naïve action. Moon-consciousness fluctuates, at times bright and white, at times dark. It is periodic, reactive and, in men, it shows itself in variations of mood and emotion.

Orpheus refused this world when he refused the body. It was but a trap or cage for the soul. Yet it was through the body that his emotional femininity tore him apart. This means, in part, that the life of the body also belongs to the feminine principle. The vegetative, nature-like anima figure seems—in analytical experience—to be intimately connected with the vegetative involuntary nervous system, its moods and fluctuations and reactions, its inaccessibility to direct control by the will, by the voluntary nervous system.

The development of the body does not mean muscle-building. It does not mean tanning and treating it as if it were an object, or perfecting it as a trained animal in techniques of judo or karate or sexual expertise. We may recall a distinction often forgotten between flesh and body. The flesh is the ego's opposite and secret companion. Mental attitudes of the flesh produce mental-sex, ego-sex and pornography, and the image of ourselves as well-trained, vitamin-enriched meat. The ego and the mind look down on the flesh figuratively, just as we look down literally over ourselves externally with our eyes.

The body, on the other hand, may be considered the physical parallel to the psyche, just as flesh is to mind. The mysteries of the immaculate conception, incarnation, miraculous acts, crucifixion, and resurrection all turn on the enigmatic relationship of flesh and body. So, too, do the problems of psychosomatic medicine. Our contemporary symptoms force us to enter the flesh in a new way, through the psyche, inwardly, symbolically. Thereby we transform what is merely organic into a meaningful system of body living within the flesh. The body as a place of fantasy can far exceed the capacity of the flesh and can drive it to breakdown, for the body's range of appetitive possibility is immense. In body fantasies we can be gargantuan. On the other hand, discrepancy between body and flesh also shows, for instance, in young inhibited people with neurasthenic complaints. Flesh is in order, sound, and strong, but the fantasy of the body is cramped. They are unable to go out and solve their problems in the streets; attempts to accomplish this directly in the flesh often results in painful failure. But the body can be kindled and educated into life through its awakening to and by inner moods, fantasies, and female images.

In psychosomatic disturbances the flesh seems directed not by its own physiological laws, but by something yet subtler which is accessible to consciousness through inner psychological understanding rather than through outer observation. Psychosomatic medicine is a happy reappearance of the ancient religious doctrine of the "subtle body" and the "animal spirits." This doctrine was the basis of Eastern, Arabic, and Western psychology and medicine until the nineteenth century. It held that the organs and functions of the flesh are at the service of the spirits of the soul (animal spirits), a principle which was a union of incommensurables, a "subtle body." As both an immaterial spirit and a physical reality, it is a conception similar to the paradoxes we find today in the half-psychic, half-physical explanations of psychosomatic medicine which refer to "unconscious dynamisms," "emotional stress," or the language I have used here, "the imagination of the body."

As consciousness moves away from identification with the mind and ego, becoming broader and more feminine in its receptivity and self-intimacy, the flesh as well transforms into body consciousness. (We find ourselves more difficult to treat only medically, more sensitive to pharmacological agents.) Body consciousness begins with the inner experience of the flesh, the actual incarnation of our humanity in warmth and joy and ease and rhythm and being present here and now, physically close to ourselves, to our symptoms and sensations, and to the physical reality of others. Out of the stable of one's own hunted and exhausted flesh, one's own rejected physical self, asinine and dumb as an ox, the new body is born and then come the kings bringing gifts.

This descent to the flesh and its transformation into body, this movement inward toward a mystery, sacred and connected to the feminine, we find described poetically in D. H. Lawrence or pictorially in Rubens, where fascination by the flesh is for the sake of body. Another image is Paul's: "your body is a temple . . . So glorify God in your body."

This way to the body is through the unconscious rather than through the conscious mind, which too often tends to stand apart from it, regarding it as an object, albeit a precious one—yes, even "mine," but unfortunately not the real "me," somehow still an "it." Then the flesh and its life become more compelling, so that the more we are cut off from it, the more it fascinates us, autoerotically to draw our attention back into it. The natural anima, that tawny-skinned swimmer, the playful and cat-like one, and the moods and fantasies she construes, lead one downward into animal warmth, physical moods and sensations. The cramped symptoms, the worry over the flesh as object and what can go wrong with "it," at last have a chance to fall away.

The longing to become whole again, healed in flesh and resurrected into body, does not have to be achieved through an outer forbidden sexual union, even though this is frequently the way a man feels he can be redeemed, his body given back to him again. In fact, the deepest intimacy with his own physical feelings is expressed in the psyche of a man by the image of the "sister" with whom an outer sexual union is forbidden. Yet as accompaniment to these crucial emotions the psyche insists upon the sister-image. Behind the attraction to the forbidden woman is the fascination of the "sister." To take her only reductively as infantile incestuous desires distorts her deepest meaning. Again, what is prohibited in the outer world may be a compelling necessity for the inner. Jung says: "Whenever this instinct for wholeness appears, it begins by disguising itself under the symbolism of incest. . . ."[4] My sister has my father and my mother, and my upbringing. We share the same secrets. She is of my blood and bone. My sister is me—but feminine. To unite with her is to enter myself, fertilize myself, for "incest is union of like with like. . . ."[5] She evokes in me familiarity and union with my own blood. Just as distance increases sexual polarity constellating my masculinity as sexual maleness, so fusion with her gives me my feminine identity. She awakens the original image of wholeness before the early wounds of childhood split good from bad, ego from Self, body from flesh, male from female. Through her I can be reconciled in love to my own physical nature. The sister is primordial love, no longer regressive toward the mother, but within my own generation. My sister is my equal who feels the same toward me, her brother. "How sweet is your love, my sister, my bride!" "O that you were like a brother to me . . . ." "Open to me, my sister, my love, my dove, my perfect one. . . ."

The approach to the body is similar to the approach to the dream. Both provide ways of developing the inner connection and expanding psychic reality. I can befriend the body as well as the dream, giving value, trust, and charity

[4] *The Psychology of Transference* (London and New York, 1954), p. 262.
[5] *Idem.*, p. 218.

to its impulses and needs. As only an expert can interpret a dream, so only a physician can diagnose the flesh; but both dream and body can be befriended. Befriending the dream affirms psychic reality by giving it feeling. Befriending the body is the fundamental yea-saying to physical life as a temple or vessel of something trans-physical. And this intimacy and familiarity with the body by creeping down into it and listening to it from within is the necessary counter-pole to activation of the unconscious in fantasy and dream. Without the two together, and together always, we easily slide into the old Kantian mistake of overvaluing mental contents, taking them as the only expression of the psyche which in idealist philosophy cannot be touched. Whenever the **physical** is devalued, something is being done against the **feminine** side. Incarnation, psychologically witnessed, is the feeling of life in the flesh. Resurrection of this flesh, from a psychological view, refers to the transformation of flesh into body, parallel to the transformation of egotistic will and rationality into psychic consciousness. This transformation refers also to the maturing of the body within the aging flesh. Even while submitting to the irreversible process of aging, one moves forward with the changes of maturing. Despite the ugliness of aging one feels more grateful and becomes more graceful, that is, "full of grace," which also means that the body is the place of grace. Again, grace is a feminine virtue and again the descent of this grace depends upon the prior descent into the femininity of flesh and its redemption as body.

In serving the feminine, in letting the feminine rule, there is one essential caution. Hercules serves Omphale only after the twelve labors are done, and Ulysses abides with Circe only after the ten years in battle are passed. A certain masculine position must evidently have already been won. Could this mean that first there must be an ego that has accomplished something? If so, it implies that one is best to be past mid-life, otherwise one has too little awareness, too little strength, and the ego abandons its position too easily. Then it is no sacrifice, no real reorientation. Then it is merely a regressive serving of the Mother, separation from whom was the aim of all the labors and the battles.

I do not believe that the religious moment is something altogether different from what we have been unfolding in this chapter, or from what we have been going about in all these pages. Wherever we shift God's position, whether He be the God within, or the God absolutely outside and above, or the God below as the ground of being, or the God among wherever two or three are gathered, or whether we are all in God and can never despite our frenzied exercises be lost to Him—wherever we would assign Him His place, the religious moment is an experience and that experience takes place in the psyche. Our task is perhaps less to search for and locate God, and more to prepare the ground so that He may descend from the heights as the dove plummets, or arise from the depths, or be revealed through personal love.

The ground is prepared by insearch, by courageously reclaiming the lost areas of the soul, where it has fallen into disuse and disease. It is further prepared by separating the strands of the shadow and containing in consciousness the tensions of moral perplexities, so that our actions are less like actings-out and more like acts. The personality that cannot contain itself, that falls into bits should the ego be abandoned, that has no other light but that held together by the will, is hardly the ground for a religious moment. Even if God be love, that love can shatter us if our wounds from early human loves are fragilely stitched together. Can the personality that has not taken into account in one way or another the unconscious, the shadow and the anima, be a vessel to hold a divine force? Does it not succumb too readily to the demonic inhumanity of the collective outer world or the collective unconscious?

The religious moment as described in traditional accounts is a vivid intense realization, transcending ego and revealing truth. Just this is also at what analysis aims. The truth which can be experienced there goes beyond the causal truth of oneself: the banalities of how I got this way and who is to blame and what must I do now. Analysis moves toward the larger truth of coherence, toward intimations of immortality, how my person fits into the larger scheme of fate. These revelations, by opening one door to my emotional center, illumine one corner of the darkness. This truth is also love since it gives the sense of belonging and attachment to one's own ground.

If the main shadow of counseling is love and if counseling lies in its shadow, then our work will depend on love's "perfection." Love, as *agape,* means "to receive," "to welcome," "to embrace." Perhaps the perfection of love begins through faith in and work on the feminine within us, man or woman, since the feminine ground is the embracing container, receiving, holding, and carrying. It gives birth and nourishes and it encourages us to believe. This ground welcomes us home to ourselves just as we are. I do not know how better or how else we can prepare for the religious moment than by cultivating, giving inner culture to, our own unconscious femininity. For the religious moment to touch us at least the ground can be worked and opened, within the range of our individual human limits.

Zurich and Moscia
1965/66

Postscript

A CRITICAL REVIEW

OF HIS BOOK

BY ITS AUTHOR

THE LAST paragraph of the 1967 Preface warns against "the gradual replacement of 'soul' by 'psyche.'" This caution, now that we are moving fast through the nineties, could as well be turned the other way. Since the sixties, 'Soul' has become a best-seller word, attesting both to easy popularization and to an urgent need in the populace for something it cannot locate. Indeed, the classic term 'psyche' which stands for that third realm between body and spirit seems to be fast dissolving into these old aggrandizing claimants. On the one hand, psyche has been taken over by body-work, from the proponents of Prozac psychiatry and bio-genetics to the weightwatches, huggers, hyper-ventilators, and cranial manipulators. On the other, a spiritualized New Age has evaporated psyche with pastel prescriptions for serenity, vacuity, and global consciousness. This spiritualized sense of psyche in the name of soul has taken a well-traveled road toward inoffensive gentrification since I first tried to reclaim the word for psychology in 1964 (*Suicide and the Soul*), rooting 'soul' less in pastoral and theological history than in current usage in soul food, soul music, and soul brother.

Since soul is the main theme of this book, the term first needs placing within the time of the book's writing, the sixties. Then 'soul' was introduced to refresh psychology, not to lull it with transcendence and transformation, because psychology then was largely an autocratic province of the objectivist scientistic establishment. Hence the title of the book, *Insearch*, as a challenging antidote to research.

Besides the opposition to research, the title states clearly the book's idea of soul—that it is an interiority and that it is lost. These are two big assumptions, and they determine the course of the book's brief and therefore the thrust of this critique.

The first assumption—that soul is lost—shares the nostalgia of Jung's 1933 title (in English), *Modern Man in Search of a Soul*, and so "insearch" is a play on that book thirty years earlier. Furthermore, Hillman's subtitle repeats Jung's 1937 Terry Lectures at Yale, *Psychology and Religion*. Right from the start, *Insearch* presents itself as a recapitulation of the Jungian tradition of soul-making, Hillman walking in Jung's shoes. Even if he can't fill them, both Jung's and his are shaped on similar lasts, and go off in the same direction: soul is lost, can be found through psychotherapy; psychotherapy is akin to a religious activity or requires an awakening of a religious attitude, function, or discipline.

Once we have assumed that the soul is lost, several consequences follow. First, our days and nights will be affected by emptiness, mourning, and longing, like a chronic 'dis-ease.' We will feel lost to and in the world, clutching, demanding, searching, and hoping for a supportive Miriam or a good shepherd to lift us up and succor us in our abandonment.

128

From the evidence of the nineties, the premise of Hillman in the sixties and of Jung in the thirties that the soul is lost is correct. The practices of both psychotherapy and pastoral counseling verify that depression, victimization, and feelings of isolated abandonment and consequent attempts at recovery by means of soulful personal relationships are the content of patients' and parishioners' complaints. One and the same myth of a lost soul, either abandoned or damned, has turned the head of therapy backwards to recovery of soul from the early life of childhood and turned the head of religion backwards to evangelical fundamentalism and saving the soul from perdition through the conversion of rebirth.

But what comes first, the chicken or the egg? The *actual* loss of soul or the *myth* of loss of soul? Does the myth derive from the actualities, and therefore is not a myth but a logical conclusion, a hypothesis? Or, does the evidence supporting the hypothesis derive from the myth? If we assume the soul is lost, will we not explain our dilemmas in terms of that basic assumption. For instance, if we assume the earth to be flat, will we not account for the sunset in terms of the sun's going down under the earth to rise again the next day?

Perhaps, neither chicken nor egg. An altogether different metaphor: numbness and dumbness. Or, to use a nineties term that goes back to the nineties of the *last* century and Freud— denial. Maybe the soul is right here at hand, not abandoned, not lost at all. We just haven't noticed. We've been looking in the wrong place. How curious this paranoid tendency of the mind: when we don't see something we are looking for, we at once imagine it to be stolen, hidden, or lost. Why not instead imagine that the fault lies in our eyesight, that the thick glasses we are wearing are too far-sighted to see what's close at hand.

Now this book, *Insearch*, is a masterful essay about looking in the wrong place. Insearch: searching inside. Inside yourself, inside your moods and feelings, inside your dreams and relationships. This move inside is presented consistently, carefully, and feelingly through each of the four regions of interiority covered by the chapters. But it all stays inside; no door is opened to the world. The author doesn't even get to the window.

What's missing is the inside "out there": in the trees, in the finches and squirrels in the trees, in the soil and stones, and even in the panes of glass that you see through to the trees, the squirrels, and the stones. Maybe the soul isn't lost; it's just elsewhere, otherwise engaged. Maybe it's more involved with the way of the world than with your path of individuation. Maybe it's not too concerned with human relationships, human moods, human personality development. From the evidence of archaic peoples and ancient philosophies, soul was never altogether in the human arena. But its absence from that arena doesn't mean that it's lost.

Why are we numb to the soul in things other than our selves? Why are we dumb to speak to and with this soul out there? Is it really lost, or fiercely defended against? What investment has our culture in its locus only inside us, and is "search" with all its collaterals like 'journey,' 'trials,' and 'guides' the right term for reestablishing connection? Might it not be far simpler just to step outside, or walk around your room, and do what the Psalmist said: "O taste and see." Soul is in, or *is*, the very first matter to hand.

Because of this denial of the world, the book is driven by a relentless engine of moral earnestness. It really does want to search out the soul from inside each person, and it prescribes ways of doing this. Could there be a psychological insight here? Do we become desperately earnest when we are out of touch, because the reverse seems evident—when we are "with it" and "in the zone" things lighten up, the shots come easy, and life floats quite pleasurably.

The moral earnestness has another source: the book's parasitical relation with Christianity. (It was originally composed from lectures given at a New England theological school and to Midwestern ministers at a post-Easter pastoral counseling conference.) Without the upright oak of Christian thought, this book could not stand on its own. The premises that the soul is lost and must be found (saved) together with the denial of the world as ensouled are particularly basic in Christian eschatology. Also Christian is the book's conviction that moral work on oneself benefits the soul and is a main road to its salvation.

The vertical direction of the first chapter and the downward depth into the feminine ground of the last chapter turn attention away from what is around us, the actual life shared with the environment, to what's above and below—the characteristic foci of Christian eschatology, Heaven and Hell. This emphasis upon the two poles above and below leaves the great wide world as mainly a dangerous ladder between them, a ladder from which one may fall at every step. The world is thus turned from a place of beauty and learning into a horizontal battlefield of moral struggle. To climb the ladder and recover your soul, you must make athletic efforts. That enigmatic phrase from Heraclitus, "the way up and the way down are one and the same," and which is repeated often by Jung, determines the path for the soul and its insearch; and this phrase also indicates that despite what the author insists about darkness and demons encountered on the way down and how different that direction is from going up, the aim is nonetheless interchangeable with Heaven.

If the way up and down are one, then demons are merely angels of another sort. Why didn't the author twist that famous Heraclitean phrase delineating the soul's path (since twisting old ideas is his special delight) to say instead: the way out and way in are one and the same? Then deepening into self and attending to world are the same. This twist would result in an insearch that is an outreach at the same time.

That the way up to Heaven is a downward and inward *via* also accounts for Hillman's very clear and very strong chapter on the Shadow, where shadow too is conceived in accordance with the Christian tradition—i.e., it is a moral issue and a "problem." He discusses shadow using the rhetorics of evil, conscience, love, internalization, conflict, and other standard concepts of the Christianized imagination of shadows.

This Christian framework for the author's discussion of shadow places his analysis in the realm of moral philosophy rather than in depth psychology. If it were a *psychological* shadow, then we would be examining our theories of perception and cognition (more in the manner of Wittgenstein), raising doubts about our senses, what they are selecting, ignoring, distorting. How do the patterns of our thought determine the world we behave in and adapt to? How narcissistic, even solipsistic, are our theories; what are the roots of our subjectivity? If our interest were a *psychological* shadow, our attention would also be turned to language and the shadows of our discourse (more in the manner of Derrida). We would have to inquire into the way in which our discourse about shadow determines the nature of shadow. How shadow as a concept acts as a verb, shadowing our language. And we would ask such questions as how do the idea of shadow and the language of shadow as a moral problem invent the kind of shadow that we struggle with.

Again if our interest were in a *psychological* shadow, we would be obliged to use the eye of psychopathology. We would want to know about character defects, psychopathic lacunas, the missing pieces of personality inventory, and the heightened spikes of repetitive propensities that seem collective, congenital, and everlasting, and which are more usefully conceived as structural karmic data (givens) than as moral problems to be repented, mastered, and transformed.

I am concluding, thirty years after the book was conceived, that the entire shadow issue so basic to Jungian psychology and therapy is a by-product of its Christian moral theology and does not actually face the psychological issue which shadows all Western psychic life, that is, keeps the Western Christianized psyche in the dark about the world and *its* soul, *its* isolation, *its* sadness and abuse. And so we are also naively in the dark about the shadows concealed in the world—its stubborn secretiveness, its predation and cruelty, its amoral ambivalence toward human beings, its manic profligacy and bipolar extremes, its eruptive violence. Without this shadow awareness extending into the world, it becomes good gray Gaia, good ol' Mother Nature all over again.

Ever since the beginnings of depth psychology, awareness of shadow meant lifting repression, that is, opening the cellar door and releasing the sexual libido and its images from internalized collective censorship. Depth psychology is always up against the deeply rooted, stalwart morality of Christian repression, and we have still not been able to untangle the psychological vine from the moral tree. To lift repression at once invites fantasies of "permissive behavior," so that descriptions of shadow in psychology become inseparably entwined with problems of morality in religion.

It doesn't have to be that way. Lifting repression from unconsciousness may have no content whatsoever, neither sexual, nor moral, nor any preordained set of specific feelings or images. Lifting repression *psychologically* (in distinction to morally) means recognizing the fateful and ever-present unconsciousness in all consciousness, that whatever consciousness casts light upon at once creates a shadow. The moment we see more clearly, we become more blind and cannot see behind what we see, the other side of what we see. Seeing and not seeing go together, concurrently, co-relatively. Or, as Jung said years ago, the taller the tree, the longer the shadow. Tho' that shadow seems cast by the tree and in the shape of the tree, it originates in light.

The very light that would search out the soul from its interior hiding cannot help but see through a glass darkly. I use the well-known Christian metaphor here because the cataracts that cloud our ability to see the soul as it is actually and continually displayed by the world are Christian. (Our unconscious shadows are not simply sexual, sinful, and moral; these we know about too well to be psychological shadows. These have become conscious to us as members of the wide media public. Who is not conscious of hired assassins, jealous murder, sexual violence, callous corruption, ethnic fanaticism, assaultive incest going on in the tabloid pablum as part of current affairs each sixty minutes of every forty-eight hours—and not only in the rich and famous but in ourselves as statistical pieces of the collective populace.) The moral notion of the shadow centers our insearch on ourselves, keeps psychology locked in subjectivity, and prevents us from seeing the soul of the world.

Shadow is thus not a moral issue only, or only one of cleansing evil from the heart so that love may flow from its springs. Shadow is the penumbral life that lives with life as the never-ceasing darkening of the light in every search, a darkening of the light of certainty, the light's own sense that however an "I" searches for soul, that same "I" is inherently biased against the object of its searching and therefore biases the methods it employs for its search. Shadow both keeps us searching and prevents us finding. It is the obstruction that does not want to find what it's looking for. Embedded in the very consciousness that is the instrument of our insearch, shadow is the unconsciousness of consciousness itself. Reframing the shadow question from morality to psychology results in different feelings regarding shadow, a different sense of discomfort than the guilt of moral wrong-doing. The basic psychological question at the bottom of all shadow issues is the question which has set the course for the psychoanalytic adventure since its inception—where is the unconscious now; how is it affecting consciousness; how can I perceive these effects and alter them (i.e., become conscious of unconsciousness)?

This psychological shadow cannot be defined by qualities of evil and sin; it does not consist in attributes of personality

134

that have been suppressed or repressed. Shadow is an inevitable necessity of the human condition, an indelible psychological fact of all perception and all behavior. No mirror reveals it, no insight dispels it. Like ancient Greek fate that keeps us mortal, flawed, humanely limited, shadow guards us from the *hubris* of blindly trusting our own awareness, and as such, shadow is a blessing. Perhaps it is a gift from Hades.

By shifting to a psychological approach to shadow, we free shadow of its "ego-problem." We free the idea from moral obligation, expressed by the Jungian term "integration." Integration of the shadow, as Chapter III suggests, is no easy matter. By saying it is not easy, the chapter still speaks the language of heroic Christianity, the rhetoric of a heroic ego, a good soldier or servant, doing his duty in a moral *agon*. The classic Jungian approach, like that of Christian morality, is to confront the devil of *superbia*, acknowledge our sins, repent. The exercises of integration supposedly take down the ego's arrogance, not merely by confronting the devil, but by recognition—and here's the Jungian twist—that *you* are the devil. That he lurks in your own breast and can be found out by diligent insearch. Result of integrating the shadow? A darkened person, yet one more chastened, rounded, and complete—if not eschatologically saved, at least psychologically improved.

An "ego-problem" nonetheless remains inasmuch as the integrative efforts are made by none other than the ego. Ego feels guilt; ego lifts the repression and recognizes the faults and sins; ego atones and is redeemed. In all this *agon*, there remains the heroic conviction that moral effort can alter psychological nature.

But once the whole discussion of shadows shifts off its moral base, then ego is not at personal fault for a collective cultural numbing which comes with the Christian territory. A collective problem is not an ego fault.

Only likes cure likes: moral problems may be moved by moral means; but moving the psychological shadow calls for psychological means, i.e., insights into the shadow of ideas, language, and psychopathology—the three components so basic to a psychological shadow. Or, to say this in another way and give it a twist from Wolfgang Giegerich's critiques: the psychopathological shadow at its fundamental level is neither evil, devil, nor lovelessness, but the *shadow of psychology itself*, the psychopathological lacuna in its theory that neglects the soul out there. For, even after the classic Jungian program of shadow integration has been fulfilled and the more whole person has been formed, the finch still chirps in the tree outside, altogether neglected by the shadow integration. The finch and the tree are eternally excluded (damned? lost?) by the logic of psychology. They do not belong to the inner society. They cannot be integrated by the soul work as insearch. They must be neglected by psychology as it defines itself. Like all the rest of the world, they must remain in shadow.

Hillman writes:

> . . . darkness means neglect. And it is the neglected elements which appear in the shadow. . . .
>
> The cure of the shadow is on the one hand a moral problem, that is, recognition of what we have repressed, how we perform our repressions, how we rationalize and deceive ourselves, what sort of goals we have and what we have hurt, even maimed, in the name of these goals. On the other hand, the cure of the shadow is a problem of love. How far can our love extend to the broken and ruined parts of ourselves. . . . How far can we build an inner society on the principle of love, allowing a place for everyone? (pp. 75–76)

What do we hurt and maim, and what do we not love once we extend the limits of our search beyond the "inner society"? The Christian reply and the Kantian reply based on it is: our neighbor. Do unto others. But here, too, "others" remains limited to the human. Are the finch and the tree not also neighbors? As for animals, the great Christian educator and theologian J. H. Cardinal Newman wrote:

> We have no duties towards brute creation; there is no rela-
> tion of justice between them and us. . . . They can claim
> nothing at our hands; into our hands they are absolutely de-
> livered. We may use them, we may destroy them at our pleasure,
> not our wanton pleasure, but still for our own ends, for our
> own benefit and satisfaction, provided we can give a rational
> account of what we do. (*Sermons Preached on Various Occa-
> sions*, VI, London, 1858)

To press further than animals, what about the soil and the stones, the rivers and seas, or the food we set on our tables and things we buy for our closets. Are these "others"? Have we a moral obligation to them? Before they may be considered to belong within the circle of our love or to be recognized as suffering possible harming and maiming, the shadow of psychological theory would have to be acknowledged and removed from them. For clearly they have been ignored *per definitionem* from our anthropocentric insearch. Only by turning to them and listening to them as subjects can we find out from them the extent of their disease.

This critique of the vertical direction, together with its nostalgia for a lost soul and neglect of the soul's presence in the horizontal world, belongs to today—to the nineties when the larger danger seems to be loss of the larger world. A hindsight critique distorts historical realities, belaboring a book for what it failed to do rather than appreciating it for what it did do, and still is able to do.

And, there is nothing "wrong" with the book, providing we recognize its Christian foundations. As such it represents a classic example of the Jungian introverted and Reformation-based, even pietist, approach which follows the path of an individuation process through four chapters as four stages: (1) entering therapy and a therapeutic relationship as the beginning of every insearch; (2) recognizing unconsciousness and that Jungian therapy inevitably invites religious issues; (3) struggling with the shadows of the objectionable and repressed; and (4) finally enlarging inward receptivity, imagination, and feeling which classical Jungian theory calls "the feminine" or anima. Even in their fourness these chapters conform with the main line of Jungian psychology with its roots in Christian spiritual progress of the soul toward salvation and in reformational *Bildung*, or cultivation of the inner person.

The program or Pilgrim's Progress consists in the identification with suffering, the virtue of work, the honesty of confrontation, and the eventual redemption through love, or anima. ("Anima," as described in Chapter IV, combines soul, love, the feminine, and religion in one satisfying solution. This was written prior to the author's later deconstruction of the term in his 1973 and '74 *Spring* articles and expanded into a book, *Anima: An Anatomy of a Personified Notion*, 1985.)

The mid-sixties was not yet a fully violent time. Such hopeful softness belonged to flower-power and all you need is love. Black and white marching the dream together, migrations back to the earth and to Haight-Ashbury—inklings of an Aquarian age limned only distantly against the dark doings in Southeast Asia and Southeast USA. And so the two sharply ironic critiques also belong to this period and reflect Hillman's wariness about the unthinking optimism and overboard feelings of the sixties' counter-culture movement.

First, his emphasis on wising-up about love:

> Love can be taken at many levels, and the consulting room of the analyst or the pastoral counselor will be the ending place for many a love in which people have given themselves to the uttermost, met the ultimate, with noble intentions and deep feelings, asserting that their love was the ground of their exis-

tence, their sense of homecoming, even their experience of God and transcendence—and yet it all went wrong, dreadfully, horribly, sometimes suicidally wrong. . . .

Love romanticized is a sweet-cheat answer to the dried and technical world. . . . as analysts and counselors know, in the noble aim of deep personal love when we would give our uttermost love we give our nethermost beast to someone else to keep for us.

To presume that every experience of love is Love of the Divine Ground of Being, to imagine that deep personal meaningfulness surmounts the pitch and hurdles of love's intricacies and can be the criterion for justification of unsanctified love, to be cozened into love by a philosophy which neglects its fearfulness (for if God is love, then the beginning of wisdom is the fear of love). . . . (pp. 80–81)

Second, the discussion of sexuality and the sixties' "sexual revolution" as fantasy:

I can indeed look upon an object with desire and cultivate that desire, watching it, feeling it, letting its imaginary possibilities run away with my mind, entertaining its delight, without acting it out. A separation may be made between inner and outer, between desire contained in the subject and desire acted out upon the object, between the left-hand of feeling-filled images and needs and the right-hand of desirous demands. Thus it is the right eye and the right hand which offend and are to be sacrificed (Matthew 5:29), for the right side is the side of action. Fantasy leads straight into action only when there is not enough space between idea and impulse, when the inner realm is so cramped that nothing can be contained for long. . . . Fantasy may take its instigations from outer events and then manipulate those events in mind, but its realm is purely imaginary. So, too, the lust and covetousness are imaginary—that is, they are psychic dynamisms, impulses of the soul, which would be ludicrously short-circuited were they directly to enter the world. These impulses appear not so much in order to be sated as appetites by action, but to create the inner realm, to enlighten the soul's insights, to give it play and dimension, to set it free from concrete limitations upon the possible, and thus to deepen and enrich its scope of experience.

As was said above in Chapter III, the real revolution in the soul is not in itself sexual. The human sexual instinct is widely plastic and provides energy for changes in consciousness all through psychological history. If one may read the trend of collective events through the particular experiences of individuals, the deep change now going on is merely carried by sexual fantasies as psychic dynamisms, the intention of which is ultimately a revivification and expansion of psychic reality. (pp. 116–17)

In sum, because of its univocal call to the vertical direction, down and in, *Insearch* still claims attention, still holds value. Since his *The Dream and the Underworld*, Hillman shows one can indeed go down and in without going Christian. In other words, insearch is even more a necessity today as long as we are aware of its overdetermination by Christian signposts which keep pointing upward even while we descend. And that awareness is precisely the aim of this Postscript: to separate insearch from its Christian determination.

As much today as when it was first written, "insearch" still plays off the outer objectivist focus of most psychology and its research. Insearch follows feeling and fantasy, not facts as found in studies, reports, experiments, statistics, and cases. It claims there is as much to be discovered in reflection, insight, imagination, and dream as in a thorough "review of the relevant literature" or in longitudinal and double-blind studies supported by grants from the NIMH (i.e., taxpayers) based on approved experimental design. Insearch is even more valid today as the psychiatric and psychological establishments succumb to the pharmaceutical account of the soul, the crass materialism which reduces soul to a "dysfunctional" body, a mere epiphenomenal whistle emanating from and depending upon the state of the kettle. The book's ultimate reply to research is fantasy. And the hard labor equivalent to the tedious, repetitive, and frustrating effort of research is the struggle of imagination.

> The phase beyond fantasy is imagination, which is the work of turning daydreams and fantasies into scenic inscapes wherein one can enter and which are peopled with vivid figures with whom one can converse and feel, and touch their presence. This, then, would be psychological insearch. Such imagination costs great effort. The work of converting fantasy into imagination is the basis of the arts. It is also the basis for the new steps we take in life, since the visions of our personal futures come first as fantasies. (p. 117)

Also by JAMES HILLMAN from SPRING PUBLICATIONS

ANIMA: AN ANATOMY OF A PERSONIFIED NOTION

Anima and Eros, Anima and Feeling, Anima and the Feminine, Anima and Psyche, Mediatrix of the Unknown, Integration of the Anima, etc.—ten succinct chapters, accompanied by relevant quotations from Jung (on left-hand pages facing Hillman's essay), which clarify the moods, persons, and definitions of the most subtle and elusive aspect of psychology and of life. Illustrated. (188 pp.)

SUICIDE AND THE SOUL

A classic introduction to the *experience* of depth psychology—for analyst, patient, and anyone having to meet questions of suicide. Although ostensibly a practical treatise on suicide, it opens into the profound differences between the medical model of therapy and one that engages soul. Since the book's first publication in 1964, it has enjoyed wide recognition in many languages as a teaching text. (191 pp.)

LOOSE ENDS: PRIMARY PAPERS IN ARCHETYPAL PSYCHOLOGY

Twelve papers and talks, including: "Abandoning the Child," "Nostalgia of the Puer Eternus," "Precursors of Archetypal Psychology," "Betrayal," "Schism," "Masturbation Inhibition," and "Failure and Analysis." Affirms the reality of the psyche and affords an example of subtle, nuanced psychological thought. With notes and / or bibliography appended to each essay. (209 pp.)

INTER VIEWS: CONVERSATIONS WITH LAURA POZZO ON PSYCHOTHERAPY, BIOGRAPHY, LOVE, SOUL, DREAMS, WORK, IMAGINATION, AND THE STATE OF THE CULTURE

A vivid, free, exploratory dialogue that follows the imagination ruthlessly and lovingly pursued down the alleys of the modern city, the soul's twisted pathologies, and the mazes of love. Extraordinary, yet practical accounts of active imagination, of writing, of daily work, and of symptoms and sufferings in their relation with loving. The only biography of Hillman's life, the book is as well a radical deconstruction of the interview form itself, even though one reads along as if in a café conversation with Hillman explaining his life and thought. Index. (198 pp.)

ARCHETYPAL PSYCHOLOGY: A BRIEF ACCOUNT

Traces the intellectual ancestry of archetypal psychology, assembles its literature, and clarifies the root metaphors governing its practice. Concise discussions of Jung and Corbin, soul-making, polytheism, Neoplatonism, the soul–spirit distinction, Greek myth and psychopathology, and other topics. Includes a bibliography of relevant publications, as well as a complete checklist of all James Hillman's writings through January 1993 (103 pp.).

For a catalog, write:
Spring Publications, Inc. • 299 E. Quassett Rd. • Woodstock CT 06281
To order, call:
Publisher Resources • 800–937–5557

DATE DUE

SEP 1 2 2000			
GAYLORD			PRINTED IN U.S.A.